SEX and the Single Soul

JACK W. HAYFORD

SEX and the Single Soul

Regal

From Gospel Light
Ventura, California, U.S.A.

\\ l / ,
Regal

PUBLISHED BY REGAL BOOKS
FROM GOSPEL LIGHT
VENTURA, CALIFORNIA, U.S.A.
PRINTED IN THE U.S.A.

Regal Books is a ministry of Gospel Light, a Christian publisher dedicated to serving the local church. We believe God's vision for Gospel Light is to provide church leaders with biblical, user-friendly materials that will help them evangelize, disciple and minister to children, youth and families.

It is our prayer that this Regal book will help you discover biblical truth for your own life and help you meet the needs of others. May God richly bless you.

For a free catalog of resources from Regal Books/Gospel Light, please call your Christian supplier or contact us at 1-800-4-GOSPEL *or* www.regalbooks.com.

Library of Congress Cataloging-in-Publication Data
Hayford, Jack W.
  Sex and the single soul / Jack W. Hayford.
    p. cm.
  ISBN 0-8307-3805-3 (trade paper)
  1. Sex—Religious aspects—Christianity. I. Title.
BT708.H41 2005
241'.66—dc22   2005022240

1   2   3   4   5   6   7   8   9   10   /   10   09   08   07   06   05

Rights for publishing this book in other languages are contracted by Gospel Light Worldwide, the international nonprofit ministry of Gospel Light. For additional information, visit www.gospellightworldwide.org; write to Gospel Light Worldwide, P.O. Box 3875, Ventura, CA 93006; or send an e-mail to info@gospellightworldwide.org.

Contents

Acknowledgments

When someone has nearly 50 books published with their name indicated as author, anyone who knows about writing knows that at least a dozen or more other people deserve their name on the cover too.

While my books are not "ghost" written, they are the result of a "host"—a team of gifted individuals who *inspire, instruct* and *support.*

> *Inspiring* by their encouragement and enablement, as in this case—

- The wonderful people comprising the singles' "family" at The Church On The Way; and
- The incredible support team surrounding me at The King's College and Seminary and the central offices of The Foursquare Church International.

> *Instructing* by their publishing wisdom and editorial savvy—

- The dynamic team at Regal Books, led by their creative president and his wife, Bill and Rhonni Greig, III; and supported by those who provide so much help in so many ways—Kim Bangs, Deena Davis and a multitude of others who make Regal such a strong force for God and for good.

> *Supporting* by assisting and untiringly seeing things through—

- My editorial assistant, Selimah Nemoy, whose dedication to Christ and His call on her life are her primary motivation, and whose skill and tenacity to task are pivotal to my completing projects like this; and
- My precious wife, Anna—who, along with our Lord Jesus, is my greatest supporter—filling me with faith, strength and love.

My thanks to all,
Jack W. Hayford

Introduction

I'd like to invite you to see with me a double meaning in this book's title. I've written *Sex and the Single Soul* not only to address unmarried men and women but also to address the broader scope of temptation that besets every one of us. Whether married or unmarried, widowed or divorced, we *all* stand as single souls before God. Each of us is personally accountable to Him for upholding the integrity of our walk in the midst of an increasingly perverted world.

My primary purpose for writing this book (as well as the other two volumes in the Sexual Integrity series from Regal Books—*Fatal Attractions: Why Sex Sins Are Worse Than Others* and *The Anatomy of Seduction: Defending Your Heart for God*) is not primarily because of questions people ask, although I have endeavored to answer many of them.

Nor have I written this book because I am religiously judgmental or prudishly critical of the moral confusion in our culture. *I am not.* However, no thinking person should dare be passive about our culture's moral confusion. Within reach of every one of us is the capacity for our sexuality to detonate and damage—if not destroy—our personal lives. Like plastic explosives in the hands of an untrained individual, anyone can be lured by the foolhardy notion "I'll be careful . . . I'll just do *T-H-I-S* . . ." (followed by a blast and whatever ruin it produces).

I have written this book because I have an abiding, pastoral passion for *people*—in this case, for singles, perhaps the most dynamically capable yet untapped and too seldom honored resource for world-changing influence through the Church. I long to see singles drawn into discipleship—to be met like the first disciples who were encountered at the beach where they were fishing—and to help them hear Jesus call out to them, "Follow Me!"

Yet other voices are calling, too, and they're hypnotizing a generation of singles, collegians and youth. The style of today's entertainment, of media's loose and libertine bent, of society's embrace of relativism ("anything goes"-ism) as well as its descent into hedonism ("nothing immoral is bad if it feels good") is sucking understanding out of minds and wrestling any remaining vestige of moral conviction to the floor. The result: *Death*. Bodies die from disease, marriages die from infidelity, souls die of deceit, babies die as inconveniences and a culture is destroying itself from the groin up. Sexual indulgence outside the boundaries of God's order is killing the people of our planet. (If no other evidence is needed, we must face the global HIV-AIDS epidemic—an unprecedented human disaster so often whitewashed by media who report it divorced from its primary means of infection—sexual transmission—as though it were just another form of the flu.)

So I offer this brief book, dear reader (whatever your marital status), as a book targeted on your and my great and wonderful purpose and potential in the hands of the One who invented us. He is the living, loving God who, years ago, gave life to a grand idea He has with our names on it.

Each of us as individuals—as single souls—possesses the equal potential of either (1) experiencing that grand idea under the touch of and with the blessing of our Maker, or (2) falling prey to the confusing tactics of an adversary committed to our ruin—an adversary who, more than by any other means, manipulates or distorts our sexuality to achieve that ruin.

I invite you to join me for a few pages of frankness. This isn't a long book, but I hope it might be a book that brings clarity on pivotal themes that are faced by every single soul.

Jack W. Hayford

CHAPTER 1

Applauding Singles
Every Generation's Unsung Heroes

"Pastor Jack," Margie said, "I have a big question." Her manner was intense but not pushy, her eyes expressing doubt without cynicism. There was no edginess at all to her manner or voice—nothing but clear-eyed, intelligent sensibility.

"As a single person," she said, "can I ever *truly* find and fulfill God's highest and best for my life? Sometimes I get the feeling that marriage is God's first choice for everyone—that to be single inevitably leaves a person short of God's best."

Her noticeable sense of comfort in her own identity and her uncontentious tone gave perfect credibility to her inquiry. As she continued speaking, three things became obvious:

(1) She was asking an earnest question, not an argumentative one;
(2) She was not resistant to the prospect of marrying, but neither was she of the feeling that she would necessarily do so; and
(3) Her sense of purpose and mission, both in her vocation and in her life's call as a disciple of Jesus Christ, was clearly fixed.

I listened to her closely. I cared *very* much. I was grateful for both her question and her attitude, because she was issuing an open invitation to me to answer a bevy of questions I've encountered during years of pastoring a congregation in which 40 percent of our members are singles. So let me begin with an announcement: I applaud singles!

- Single collegians and twenty-somethings who are focused on their education or beginning their careers (marriage isn't even on the table as a subject yet)
- Single parents who hold the dual potential of not only being their children's hero as they handle the demands of job and parenthood, but who are also my heroes. I witness their devotion to their kids and their diligence to their work, day in and day out
- Single *un*marrieds who have known the pain, problem or grief occasioned by a divorce, a betrayal, an abandonment or the death of a partner, yet who still choose to remain open to God's love and strength to help, His power to heal, and His presence to comfort

I love and applaud singles in any and every generation of life, and no matter where they find themselves within the spectrum of circumstances or the span that encompasses singlehood. From the outset of this book, let me assert that there isn't one of those singles who is even slightly less in God's order or potential for life fulfillment by reason of his or her being single.

> God's highest desire and design for you is not reduced, inhibited or restricted by your singleness.

Every single person needs to understand that truth. If you are reading this as a single, God's highest desire and design for you is not reduced, inhibited or restricted by your singleness.

So I begin not only by applauding singles but also by inviting you to join me in applying living truths that can maximize each single soul's potential and fulfillment, for as long as he or she is single—up to an entire lifetime.

FACING DOWN MISUNDERSTANDING

To start, let's face head-on the threat of misunderstanding one of the initial possibilities for a single person's confusion—possibly a point that contributed to Margie's question. It relates to a picture of marital union that the Holy Spirit has employed in the Word of God.

The metaphor of bridegroom and bride laced throughout Scripture is indicative of a rich relational potential founded on covenant principles and sustained by deep, selfless love. In human terms, the husband-wife relationship models for us a glimpse of the spiritual intimacy, partnership and fruitfulness God offers through relationship with Him. This offer is backed by His desire to fulfill His Bride, the Church. At every point the offer is clear and the relational meaning for you and me as disciples of Jesus Christ is promise-filled.

Still, as magnificently beautiful as the dynamic concept of bride and groom is to demonstrate God's love and commitment to every believer, I have found that the metaphor presents a challenge to dedicated single believers who wonder if that *divine* imagery somehow projects a *human* requirement for true fulfillment in life (or at least the *preferred* plan of God in order for a person to know His fullest divine favor).

Indeed, God's creational order and intent for relationship (before the disorder that occurred as a result of human sin) begins with His words regarding the first man. Of Adam, who was at that time single in the Garden of Eden, God said, "It is not good that man should be alone" (Gen. 2:18). These words might lead one to think that there is something lacking—an incompleteness or failure—in being single; but that is not the case. God's Word is specific about the pursuit, purpose and significance of a single lifestyle.

Generally speaking, while it is most common in God's order for humankind that people be married, marriage doesn't apply to every person. If there were no other argument for this assertion, the fact that *when God became flesh, He lived a single life* verifies that there is no biblical sanctification of marriage as the *only* real plan of God for a believer's life. In God's Son, Jesus Christ, we witness a single adult who lived in purity and power and who *perfectly* fulfilled God's will and plan for His life. Singleness is equally evident in Scripture as a valued lifestyle. There is no reason for anyone to minimize hopes or purpose for their life by thinking single is less than.

Every motivation that compels my ministry has consistently been to help people realize their potential as people of the Kingdom—they are incarnate expressions of the life of Jesus in the following ways: (1) of His living in them and (2) of His ministering through them. There is nothing that disqualifies a single person from that! Yet during more than five decades of pastoring, counseling and dealing with a lot of singles, I've observed the struggles that ensue among some people who do not know how to embrace their singleness. It is not necessarily that they're uneasy about being unmarried; it's the fact that even in their enjoyment of the single life, they don't have an understanding of how to embrace singleness in order to experience how productive and fulfilling God designed that state to be. Let's talk about that design.

PURPOSE, POWER AND PURITY

While it is clear that this book confronts the challenges that face all of us who care about sustaining sexual purity (even as that value declines in our world), let me underscore my primary concern: My sights are targeted on *you*. *You,* like me, are a "single soul" who is accountable to God. His promise and hope and His mercies and grace are abundant and expansive in their reach toward each of us. My goal is to see you unleashed—to see you free in God's truth to pursue the most fulfilling life possible for you and to find purpose in your pursuits and relationships, as well as to experience God's promised power for succeeding in them all.

For *purpose and power* to be realized, however, it is essential to focus on *purity* as well, which introduces the subject of sex. This book is focused on the area of sex, not because sex sells, and not because singles are suspect, but because there is nothing more central to our humanity than our sexuality, which is essentially the reason that sexual integrity becomes so critical to our success in life. To violate this core issue of your or my being is to compromise something so basic as to stain, taint, sour or even ruin everything else. So, yes, I invite you to think with me about sex, but most of all to examine all those matters that would or could cause any one of us to fail as a single soul—that is, as an individual who is accountable to God for how we fulfill our God-given promise.

There is no trio of greater issues in life than purpose, power and purity. Purpose must be discerned, power must be received and purity must be maintained whether we are talking about an engine or a human being, an ecosystem or a race of people. Every single soul must confront these basics: (1) Do I understand my purpose? (2) Do I know my power source? (3) Do I discern what may endanger my success? Books abound concerning each of these matters; but before those books, *The Book*—the Bible—has forever been clear about them. Essentially, the Bible tells us:

- Our *purpose* is to know God (who sent His Son, Jesus, to bring us to Him) and to open ourselves to His personalized plan for each of us, which He will unfold to our understanding day by day as we learn to walk before Him in obedience to His ways.

- Our *power source* gets connected when we receive God's
  Son, Jesus Christ, whose death on the cross makes possible our forgiveness of all sin (in areas of compromise,
  selfishness and the laws of God we've broken). Christ's
  resurrection life makes possible the gift of His Holy
  Spirit to indwell us and cause us to overflow with power
  to live daily for Him and love others through Him.
- Our *purity* is not merely a religious requirement; it is
  our defense against sin's infection that will reduce
  one's quantity of life by blocking blessing and lessen-
  ing the possibility of our purpose being fulfilled.
  Holiness is not ritual behavior; it is the result of living
  a life that is undiluted (unmixed with the useless or the
  unworthy) and not deluded (undeceived by things that
  diminish our integrity).

WHY FOCUS ON SEX?

My passion in writing these pages is to clearly confront one of
today's most decimating dynamics—the confusion and corruption of human sexuality. No one will deny how readily the distortion of sexuality will infect both mental and physical purity,
thereby serving as a boomerang to waste or reduce God's power
in us and to detour or remove God's purpose for us. The inte-
gration of these three *P*s—power, purpose and purity—is too
practical to miss and the implications for our sexuality too significant to neglect taking seriously.

This book is the completion of a trilogy—a series that began
with *Fatal Attractions* and *The Anatomy of Seduction*. Because I have
felt such a distinct respect for singles, I wanted to devote one
book of the trilogy to a segment of Jesus' Church that I not only

applaud but also see as embodying an immensely dynamic potential for impacting our world for Him.

It is with *your* purpose, power and purity in mind—as well as *ours,* for we all share the same challenges—that I invite your partnership in a pursuit of sexual integrity that will protect your life purpose and also release God's living power to you and through you. With that in mind, I invite you to step with me into the Prayer Chapel of The Church On The Way for a special meeting of our congregation's single adults. Several hundred people have gathered there—brothers and sisters in Christ—to worship and to hear the Word of God as it specifically relates to their concerns.

I am presenting a forum by which those who have gathered can openly ask questions in response to the teaching and pastoral focus. In order to point people toward the pursuit of a lifestyle that wins, regardless of marital status, I want to underscore the pragmatic side of God's ways. I want to emphasize that *the life that wins, wins on the Maker's terms!* The lifestyle that prioritizes God's design and dimensions for living will be the one that experiences the fullest purpose, the most dynamic empowerment and the greatest fruitfulness and fulfillment. My hope is that you will weigh my words (really, God's Word!) and respond by saying, *I want to give myself to that—to God's will, God's ways and His wonderful working plans.* Come then, and let's look together at what it really means to be a single soul.

CHAPTER 2

Embracing Your Singleness

One Night's Happening

The room buzzed with anticipation, filled to capacity with singles of all ages—men and women who were unmarried for a variety of reasons. A mix of 25- to 30-year-olds gathered with their older brothers and sisters whose single status was the result of choice or circumstance.

As the uplifting and engaging time of worship concluded, our singles' pastor introduced me to the group and I stepped to the platform amid very warm, encouraging applause. That touched me, because I knew that they knew I loved them and believed that the real applause belonged to them!

I made a few quips about how their welcome had recharged the "old guy's" batteries, and they laughed. I added a couple of quotes from recent birthday cards I had received: "Birthdays can really sneak up on you. Of course, at your age, so could a glacier." "I'm not saying you're old, but if you were a car, I wouldn't let you park in my driveway without putting a pan under you!"

Before I transitioned into my message's theme, I related a delightful story recently shared with my wife, Anna, and me by a pair of fellow-grandparents.

Jim and Carol were visiting their daughter's family who lived in another town. After spending the night, Carol got up the next morning and went to the living room where she took a seat on the couch. Her four-year-old granddaughter, Donna, came in with a dishcloth draped over her arm like a waitress. She walked over to Carol and said, "Grandma, what do you want for breakfast?"

Seeing that her granddaughter was ready to take her order, Carol picked up on the game and said, "Well, I'll have an egg, a piece of toast and a cup of coffee."

"Okay," said Donna, who then marched off toward the kitchen. When she came back, the little girl pretended to have a tray in her arms. She set the imaginary breakfast on the coffee table and then stood back and pretended to pull out a pad to write down the total. She then tore off the imaginary slip from the pad and handed it to her grandmother.

Carol reached over as if to receive the bill from her granddaughter and asked, "Donna, how much is this?"

"Ten dollars," Donna replied.

"Ten dollars!? All I had was an egg and a cup of coffee and piece of toast," to which complaint the four-year-old responded, "Hey, I just work here!" (Laughter.)

Then I said, "You know, I feel the joy of just working here, thanking God that His Holy Spirit is at work, too; and flowing out of that, I have the privilege and joy of offering pastoral care for precious people like you."

Now, dear reader, I want to share with you what I shared that evening—what it means to embrace your singleness.

FIRST THINGS FIRST . . .

Most but not all of the singles who joined such Friday happenings are an ongoing part of our congregation or have come with someone who is. Then, as now, my primary audience is believers in Jesus Christ. But there are always some prebelievers—seekers, inquirers, honest hearts (some broken) who have not yet opened their lives to the Savior. Often people are more open to visiting or fellowshipping with a body of believers at a meeting less formal than a Sunday service.

So, at every gathering, I tell people the precious truth that applies to each and every person alive—*God loves you*. We are *all* sinners in need of a Savior, and He's given us His Son so that we might know His life, His love, His forgiveness and His purpose for us. Salvation is not only about solving the problem of our distance from God and establishing a genuine, dependable, stable relationship with the One who created us; it is also about His purpose at work in each of our lives. In relationship with our Father God, through our Savior, Jesus Christ, life begins to function in a more ordered and strategic way. God wants every one of His children to have not only His life but also His purpose and fulfillment. Salvation incorporates all those things. Jesus said, "I have come that they may have life, and that they may have it more abundantly" (John 10:10).

Like some of those dear ones gathered in that Prayer Chapel meeting, perhaps you haven't yet opened your heart to the love of God. If you are unsure about how to receive God's gift of salvation in His Son, Jesus Christ, I have provided a guide to assist you in prayer—a way to honestly come to Him and begin new life on His terms and in His love (see appendix 1). If that is what you desire to do, I encourage you to turn to the appendix now before going any further in this book. That decision will help make clear the path of purpose, power and fulfillment that I am inviting you to look at in this book, because then we can jointly see life through the eyes of its giver—the living God, our creator and ultimate lover of our souls. Go ahead, spend some minutes there—they could be the most important minutes of your life—and then we'll resume.

A SIMILAR "HAPPENING" PROVIDES OUR EXAMPLE

Believers in Jesus began to proliferate in the first century as a people who had touched life's fountainhead of meaning. The similarities between that world and ours may be drastically different technologically speaking, but in terms of living life, facing challenges, developing relationships, fumbling and stumbling or running and winning, nothing really changes from age to age.

A look at the first believers in the city of Corinth—one of ancient Greece's most successful marketplaces and one of its most corrupting cultures—provides us with a classic study in how you and I can live a real life for Christ in a world that is often counter to His best for us. The apostle Paul, in his pastoral letter to the church he founded at Corinth, responded to many of the same practical questions and concerns that people ask today. Acutely aware of the confrontations his flock was encountering in a milieu laden with habits of human exploitation, personal manipulation and ruinous sexual indulgence, Paul set forth to shepherd singles. It is refreshing to note his candor, and revealing to hear God's heartbeat pulsating through the pages of Scripture as we read:

> Now concerning virgins: I have no commandment from the Lord; yet I give judgment as one whom the Lord in His mercy has made trustworthy. I suppose therefore that this is good because of the present distress—that it is good for a man to remain as he is: Are you bound to a wife? Do not seek to be loosed. Are you loosed from a wife? Do not seek a wife. But even if you do marry, you have not sinned; and if a virgin marries, she has not sinned. Nevertheless such will have trouble in the flesh, but I would spare you. But this I say, brethren, the time is short, so that from now on even

those who have wives should be as though they had none (1 Cor. 7:25-29).

I'm using this Scripture passage as our starting place because the beloved apostle did. He begins by speaking about the social practices common in that culture; a world in which the care of daughters was highly controlled by their parents. Daughters were given in marriage; they had no choice of their own destiny. Frequently, a daughter was bartered and exploited. She would not become a loved wife, but a woman used primarily for the purpose of her husband's sexual gratification and for child-bearing. Within these kinds of marriages, there was very little that had to do with *relationship*.

When Paul mentions virgins here, he's speaking of daughters who are just that—untouched and unmarried. The question that he is responding to has to do with the father's right of the disposition of his virgin daughter's domestic destiny.

In Corinth, as people began to come to Christ, they no longer wanted to participate in that pagan barter system. Fathers began to question giving their daughters in marriage. And, as in every generation, believers lived in anticipation of the coming of the Lord, just as you and I do, causing them to wonder, *Perhaps it would be better to remain single in order to pursue what Jesus wants me to be.*

In fact, whenever the vital, healthy and growing work of the Holy Spirit is in a person's life, they will live with the anticipation of Jesus' return. The issue is, when He moves into your situation, will you be available? Will you be sufficiently mobile to do what He wants you to do with your life?

Believers at Corinth were asking Paul, "Now that we've come to the Lord, how do we handle this part of our lives?" I'm not surprised by the questions asked of Paul; the same questions have been asked of me many times in my years of pastoring.

As I noted earlier, many singles ask how they should think about their singleness. Many have admitted they were thinking about and hoping for the day they would be married. Others, having been divorced, ask about the legitimacy of their anticipating a future marriage or wonder if they ever want to be married again. Still others say they have no desire to be married right now. They ask, "Is that God telling me I should stay single and serve Him? Should I focus on my vocation, using my other time for the Lord, and not take on the responsibilities of marriage [or, some add, deny myself its joys]?"

This was what Paul addressed among the Corinthians, and the questions don't change over time. Paul's forthright response is interesting. In writing on this somewhat intimate theme, he seems hesitant to assert divine authority—even though the Holy Spirit obviously put His seal on the apostle's words by including them in the Scriptures. Nonetheless, as a single himself, the apostle asserts the strong counsel and opinion of his own heart (see v. 25).

The "present distress" (v. 26) in which they were living was a time filled with tension and pressure—a signal to them that they could expect the return of the Lord. We certainly live in such a time today—a culture loaded with every moral question mark, the increasing tension in the Middle East, the emotional uncertainties of living in a post-9/11 world and other dynamics that point to the warnings and prophecies of the Bible regarding Last Days. In a similar international environment, Paul was asked, "Are these times in which I ought to make the commitment that marriage involves?" Paul answers with clear-headed directness that he thought they would be freer if they didn't.

God's Word affirms that no one is less godly for having married, nor is anyone potentially less fulfilled for being single (see v. 28). The trouble described in regard to being married is not suggesting those problems of husbands and wives who don't get along with one another. Rather, it describes the plain demands, inconveniences and responsibilities that marriage and family life hold, "problems" that disallow the kind of freedom that single-ness more often permits. When we read that "even those who have wives should be as those who have none" (v. 29), it is not a direc-tive that spouses should not give attention to one another but that husbands and wives should not become so preoccupied with being married that they lose focus on other life issues, including their own walk with the Lord. The reason is obvious, as the text says, "the time is short"—Jesus is coming again.

The insights continue as we go deeper into the text.

> For the form of this world is passing away. But I want you to be without care. He who is unmarried cares for the things of the Lord—how he may please the Lord. But he who is married cares about the things of the world—how he may please his wife. There is a difference between a wife and a virgin. The unmarried woman cares about the things of the Lord, that she may be holy both in body and in spirit. But she who is married cares about the things of the world—how she may please her husband. And this I say for your own profit, not that I may put a leash on you, but for what is proper, and that you may serve the Lord without distraction (1 Cor. 7:31-35).

Keep in mind that Paul is addressing people of the Lord—the living Church; he is not giving counsel to people who don't know or have any interest in God's way for their lives. Thus, this pas-sage centers on the recognition that, irrespective of our domestic status, we have accountability as believers, and it is in this setting that we are presented with a key point of understanding:

The Bible casts singleness in a very positive frame of reference.

That fact sets the overarching frame of reference for finding our answer to the question, How can a single person please the

Lord? and it begins with our understanding and embracing of the greatness of God's heart for singles.

SINGLENESS IS NOT SECOND CLASS

It is crystal clear in the Scripture that singleness holds nothing less than the fullest possibilities for a joyous and God-pleasing life. Remember, Paul was speaking as a single person.

The opinion of most scholars is that Paul's having been a member of Jerusalem's Sanhedrin (70 ruling elders) meant that he had to have been married to qualify. They thus conclude that his wife had probably died and that he was a widower; although it is not impossible that she may have left him when he became a believer in Christ. So the apostle addresses singles as a single himself—a fact that doubtless added an intensely practical sense of urgency to help those to whom he ministered. He noted that by reason of *distress* (life problems and struggles) and *pressures* (to conform to social demands, not to mention immoral invitations), he chose to preserve his singleness in pursuing his life goals, rather than be encumbered with the practical challenges and needs that married life would require. He was not a misogynist—there is nothing spoken *against* marriage here; but in saying that marriage has its own fulfillment and purpose, he strongly suggests that those who are single ought to stay that way in order to serve the Lord without distraction. Again, the text doesn't issue this counsel as a demand, but the apostolic wisdom is preserved by the Holy Spirit as practical—as a single leader offering anointed, useful guidance by his own personal judgment.

Just as singleness is in no way decried in the Bible, God's Word also makes it clear that it is no less spiritual for a person to be married than it is to be single. There are undoubtedly many singles reading this book who want to be married. Perhaps you are one of them who has yearned, hoped and prayed for that special person with whom you could spend the rest of your life. If that's what you feel, let me share with you what I have learned over the years of my pastoring and counseling people: The single person who finds the quickest pathway to a fulfilling friendship that leads to marriage is one who is not desperately pursuing marriage but is passionately pursuing the will of God for his or her life. So never feel as though the desire for marriage is unworthy. The only thing that a single person can do that makes that desire unworthy is to violate God's design for our behavior before marriage or during courtship.

> In whatever way you embrace your singleness—as one convinced that, at least for the present, you are to continue as a single, or as one who anticipates marriage in the near future— the focus shifts from question marks about your domestic status to a pursuit of God's will for your life.

In whatever way you embrace your singleness—as one convinced that, at least for the present, you are to continue as a single, or as one who anticipates marriage in the near future—the focus shifts from question marks about your domestic status to a pursuit of God's will for your life. In the meantime, hold this thought: Some of the most fruitful, effective and joyous people I have pastored are singles. And it has never been because they had a negative view of marriage. The most frequent remark from such a person goes something like this: "I feel this is what Jesus is doing with my life, and I love Him!" (And, by the way, He certainly isn't deficient as an excellent life-Partner!)

No, sir! No, ma'am! Singleness isn't second-class—it is the true freedom to pursue what God has for your life *now*. And now stretches to tomorrow and the day after that until the day someone comes within that embrace, not to separate you from God but to change the nature of your singleness.

DESPERATELY NEEDED CLARITY

In writing the words "change the nature of your singleness," I intend to confront a matter that desperately needs clarity. Think on this with me.

I've often heard people speak about marriage as if it completed a person—that a marriage partner was one's other half. The problem in that terminology is that it conveys the idea that to be single is to be half a person, a concept that is a complete distortion of what the Bible teaches about the human personality.

Hear me please: You are a whole person as an individual. In terms of your fundamental person, you do not need someone else to complete you. In fact, to set forth the harsh reality that honesty recommends, *if you are looking for someone to complete you, you aren't offering the best material for a potentially healthy, fulfilling marriage.* No healthy person (not to mention one who needs healing in some areas) is going to benefit from having a less-than-complete partner who needs him or her in order to be made whole. That's why people headed for marriage need counsel—why issues need to be dealt with in advance and challenges addressed before they are discovered after the fact. Often the reason that so many marriages crumble is because those entering the union had some unattended (often unconfessed) brokenness in areas of their life.

I have done a lot of premarital counseling and have found that when men or women lack a fundamental, reasonable stability in their own right, they bring a compounding instability into a marriage.

A fruitful and happy marriage involves two reasonably whole people who come together as partners. The biblical teaching that the two shall become one is instructive, making it clear that *genuine marriage commitment involves a willingness on the part of each to make a certain sacrifice of themselves.* The benefit comes in gaining a union with someone who brings something to the partnership that you do not have on your own. Yet both partners need to make the choice to sacrifice a certain "completeness" (i.e., self-sufficiency), which they each have as individuals when they choose to become one.

While I will not further elaborate this principle here, I want to underscore two things. The first is that as a single, you are a complete person apart from ever being married. Second, a true marriage involves the surrender of something of yourself, otherwise true union is impossible. The second truth explains why some marriages never work(ed) and also why some of those who genuinely gave themselves to marriage came away from a divorce with such a deep sense of brokenness. In that regard, my years of counsel have taught me the folly of a divorced person even considering another marriage until deep healing has occurred. (I'll explain more about this later.)

Anna and I have been married for more than 50 years, and it is with great joy and confidence that I can testify to you that partnership in marriage involves a lifetime of making concessions. I'm not suggesting it isn't worth it. Neither is it learned without a will to keep on growing. But a happy marriage is composed of two people who have learned to give rather than get. The result of such giving is the marvelous relationship each receives in exchange.

Singleness is not about lacking someone else to make you whole, but wholeness does require one thing to keep it intact—it requires *becoming trustworthy*. The word "trustworthy" essentially means "faithful"—something best described in the context of a marriage but true with regard to each person's walk with Christ as well. It is a commitment that is not violated.

In that context, let me say gently but pointedly that there are people who sincerely want to live for the Lord but who have never come to the place of allowing the Lord to make them trustworthy. It's a choice—possibly the most valuable decision you could ever make besides the one to receive Jesus as Savior. But don't despair of becoming a person of full-orbed character—dependable, reliable, constant, trustworthy, faithful! God can and will work this grace in and through the fabric of your life. Paul testifies to it occurring in his own life as "one whom the Lord in His mercy has made trustworthy" (1 Cor. 7:25). In Romans 7, Paul describes how, although he was very religious, he was still unreliable. He knew about God but lacked the Holy Spirit's working the character and power of Christ in him. He explains his past as being like a person dragging his sinfulness around as though he were chained to a dead body. However, in Romans 8, he breaks into a virtual anthem of praise to God, who not only breathes His life-giving Spirit into those who welcome Him, but also removes all condemnation and leads us unto a life of faith unto *faithfulness*—becoming "more than conquerors through Christ!" (Rom. 7:37).

You can make the choice to open yourself to that grace. Although we are living in a culture in which even believers can become fixated on seeking fulfillment by things that compromise—the addictive, the toxic, the corrupt or the immoral—a living option is available to us. If, on the one hand, a believer chooses to submit to compromise, something of the life that Father God has intended for us in Christ drains out, and in its place is the unworthy and the untrustworthy. However, the opposite of "draining" is the *flowing of fullness* that the Holy Spirit brings to our lives when we let Him make us trustworthy. This isn't rocket science, dear one. Basically, by opening up to the Lord Jesus' pouring Himself into the empty spaces of your life, you will walk a sure pathway to knowing the fullness of Him! Then you can live in the wholeness that will make singleness joyous or, if you choose, prepare you with the proven faithfulness that should be brought to an altar of marriage.

SINGLENESS IS SINGLE-HEARTED

More than anything, embracing your singleness means having the capacity to give yourself to God's purpose in your life unhindered and unrestricted by other obligations, yet without being dominated by self-centeredness. It's important to learn what this means.

Some believers enjoy singleness *not* because it gives them more time to become what God intends them to be in order to make a difference in their world, but because they simply want their freedom for themselves—my life, my time, my way, my space. This so easily becomes self-centered, self-serving and self-focused—anything but Christ-like.

Paul says that he is motivated to remain single for the sake of being mobile and unhindered to do what the Lord would have him do because of "the present distress" (1 Cor. 7:26). The distress at that moment in time was a season of severe persecution of believers. His intent to remain single was to enable him to serve others, not to protect his convenience. This speaks to us today, when so many critical circumstances (distresses) in our world signal a massive opportunity for making a difference in our world if we are available and mobile (and singles are so much more so) and if we're willing to let the love of God course through our life as an expression of Jesus—reaching, touching and effecting change by His works of grace and mercy *through* us.

I am thrilled to observe so many singles opening to Christ's purpose for their lives in this way. Many, with the resources of time and financial support, go as part of a team of believers to nations around the world. They go to build, to touch people with medical aid, to minister the power of the living Jesus, to give themselves unselfishly in the interests of others.

Others do the same within their national or local boundaries. They reach out to the urban poor; they help to meet the needs of the broken and battered in their own cities; they give their time to teach Sunday School classes. It's a joy to behold—and it is exactly what the apostle Paul was talking about in our text. This behavior references something that rises in and flows through singles who single-mindedly and servant-heartedly exploit the possibilities of being single and belonging to Christ!

What Happened Next

The previous section concludes my message the night at The Prayer Chapel—a very fulfilling time of being with singles who were truly worthy of my applause. They were ordinary people with extraordinary possibilities—just like you. As I finished the teaching, I prayed and then opened the meeting for discussion. I invited written questions so that potentially embarrassing questions could be asked. The first question was from a pair of singles anticipating marriage.

> *Q: Pastor Jack, we are a couple coming from the world into Christianity, and we've been sexually intimate. Each of us were married before, but our divorces are not yet final. Since we can't get married yet, how do we handle the sexual pressure? How do we put God first in our lives and keep our relationship?*

First of all, I give wide berth to this couple because they say they are coming from the world into a new life with Jesus Christ. Therefore, I don't hold them under judgment for the life they *were* leading; it is entirely consistent with life outside of Jesus Christ. They've asked this question because they realize that a new value system is incumbent upon them if they are going to walk with God; I'm glad they feel like that. While I understand where they are coming from, nonetheless they have come to the

Lord, and in doing so, need to look at His standards.

Their first mistake (though they were walking in the world) was that they were seeing one another before they were divorced. The sad odds are that there are other believers sitting here now who also violate that. It may sound unfair and insensitive to say that, especially if the break-up of the marriage wasn't their fault, or a spouse was abusive. I'm not without compassion, but that isn't the point. The point is, What is faithful—what is *trustworthy,* leading to wholeness, as we have just noted—according to the Word of God?

The first thing this couple needs to do is stop seeing each other socially until their divorces are finalized. I didn't say they need to stop seeing each other completely—they need to build a spiritual relationship and learn to relate to each other as *persons* rather than as *bodies.* They can meet in small groups with brothers and sisters; they can even let it be known that they have a serious relationship; but for the time being they should avoid going out on dates together. During that time of true growth as *people,* rather than as "romantics," they should enter into counsel with the pastoral staff who will be performing their wedding when that time comes about. One thing this couple will hear, as any couple we counsel will be told, is that they need to plan to grow their relationship for anywhere from 9 to 12 months before marriage will be recommended.

In that light, here's an obvious question: What about the sexual pressures? Sexual pressures are no different for this couple than for anybody else. Singles are often under the illusion that married people are not also subject to sexual pressures to disobey the Word of God. Being married comes about as a result of the will of God, and if single men and women will pursue God's will, they will find the same reward; it's worth waiting for. You need to decide whether or not the Lord is taunting you with your sexuality. But of course, He's not. The gift of passion within marriage is exactly that—a gift, with great joys awaiting you if you don't open the package until marriage. Believe me, dear ones, the heart of the heavenly Father is for people to enter into relationship at the highest levels of fulfillment, including the ecstasies of marital union. But to realize that, whether people choose to believe it or not, actually requires being progressively weaned from the world's "wisdom," its propositions and confused values, and becoming disentangled from the way of the world in every aspect of sexual behavior.

Finally, this couple asked, "How do we put God first in our lives and maintain our relationship?" My answer: The same way that we put God first in all things, according to Matthew 6:33. If you will seek first the kingdom of God and His righteousness, then *all* things—including a fulfilling marriage relationship—will be added unto you. That's the promise of the Lord Jesus.

Next . . .

Q: There is a woman I love very much, but I don't find her sex-ually attractive. Should I marry her?

I cannot imagine a man or woman not feeling sexually attracted to the person they are going to marry, although it's possible that as this relationship develops, a sense of sexual attraction will too. I wouldn't argue that sexual attraction is the grounds on which people ought to marry, but if only one person in the relationship feels that, it could lead to some serious problems. Frankly, I would say that in this case, it sounds as if she is just a very dear sister to you in Christ, and that's a beautiful relationship.

It is, however, entirely possible that a person may never feel any sexual attraction, although that is certainly not the only sign that a person is being called to a single life. A person who commits themselves to a single life needs to do so out of a sense of destiny and purpose, and within that purpose choose to walk in sexual purity as a commitment to Christ, not simply because he or she may have no sexual desire.

As an aside, I don't want to leave this question without suggesting another possibility to truly complete this answer. If I were to speak personally with someone who really wanted to be married but found they had no sexual desire, I would, in my counsel, inquire whether there might be some kind of inherited or assimilated *spiritual* bondage in their life. Sometimes childhood trauma, abuses or personal indulgence of a sinful or violated past will put chains on part of the human soul—chains that Jesus Christ can break through the ministry of deliverance. That's an enormous subject in itself, some of which is covered in this book's companion volume *Fatal Attractions*. In that regard, I would also highly recommend my friend Chris Hayward's book *God's Cleansing Stream*. In any case, my recommendation would be to seek out effective ministry and counsel. As well, a prayer-pathway might be begun by utilizing the prayer guide for spiritual liberation that has been included at the end of this book (see appendix 3).

> Q: *How does a new believer who used to go to singles bars and engage in unworthy relationships fill the fellowship void?*

Serve. Volunteer. Give your life away. Jesus said, "He who loses his life for My sake will find it" (Matt. 10:39). We have a self-centered culture that is not disposed to thinking that way.

Study. Take a course in something that interests you, perhaps at a Bible college. Develop a skill. Immerse yourself in the body life of the church. Find wholesome entertainment that you can go to with brothers and sisters in Christ.

The last two questions were ones I expected to be asked, and they gave me the opportunity to close the meeting and help bring focus to sincere single men and women who ultimately were looking forward to becoming married.

Q: Can a divorced person remarry?

If you have experienced the brokenness and pain of divorce, but in your heart there is a desire to be married again, the Lord does not preempt legitimate, biblical marriage for you in your future. Let me say this, however. First, you need to get healed from whatever broke up the past. The Lord must become your preoccupying focus in order for your wholeness to be restored. Remember, when you got married, you had to give up something of yourself. And when that marriage broke up, you no longer had the original, independent wholeness you enjoyed before you were married. It takes time to grow back to being a ready-to-be-married person again. To prematurely rebound into another marriage is as futile as trying to make two amputated limbs work the same way that two connected ones work. That's the reason some people cultivate a trail of multiple broken marriages. They didn't get healed in the first place—usually because they were never truly taught or had modeled before them a genuinely substantial marriage or, at least, the concept of one.

I encourage divorced individuals who want to understand God's expectations regarding their accountability to His ways, and how to find His redemptive possibilities for realizing the possibility of a happy, fruitful marriage in their future, to do two things. First, grow within the family of a healthy congregation; second, examine God's Word as to the terms under which a divorced person may remarry. (If no resource is available to you, you may wish to obtain my 2-tape/CD album, *Biblical Perspectives on Divorce and Remarriage.* (See appendix 5.)

Q: I've never been married and am wondering if my anticipation and hope for that will ever be realized.

As you dedicate who you are as a single to the goal of making the Lord's work your focus, He will bring about the person to fulfill your hope. The world's way is fueled by desperation. Once in a while, something put together by our own design works, but it is rare. The best thing you can do is put your heart in Jesus' hands and let Him find the right heart with which to unite it. In fact, over the years, I have shared two guidelines with singles whose heart's desire is to be married.

First, *marry the heart of God.*

You may ask, "How do I do that?" We've already talked about how: Seek first the kingdom of God and then everything else will be added to you.

Second, *marry the body of the congregation where you serve.*

Give yourself to that body and be faithful to it. Pour yourself into it. If you as a single person cannot be faithful to a local congregation, you will not be faithful to a person—that is, not really, as a follower of the Savior. Faithfulness is a way of life with Him as well as with a marriage partner. Don't make any mistake about it: faithfulness isn't a "kind of" or "now and then" thing. So grow "into" a congregation and you'll grow "up" in readiness for life—including marriage. Learn to give yourself up and serve the Lord in a church family and you'll become ready to care for your own. As you do so, you will find the reward that comes from giving yourself away, not saving your life, but—as Jesus said—losing it for His sake. And that's when you find the life that wins, because it is His!

Here's an additional matter I want to address: I regularly meet singles who may have marriage in their future, as God's purpose for their life, but they are looking for some image in a person that is the epitome of excellence in ways sold by the system of this world. The Lord's spouse for you ought never to be dictated to you by a world image—that is, by a mental image you carry, lifted from the pages of the latest fashion magazine or (forgive me for mentioning it) an Internet porn site.

Finding the partner you seek for marriage begins by your seeking the Lord. The image of who your marriage partner is—how he or she looks and what he or she has—should be dictated by your discovering His will for you in this regard. God isn't calling you to marry someone you're not interested in. But you do need to learn what He has in mind—as I've observed some very wise singles do. I have watched people who, once they got rid of their own preoccupying idol of Mr. Right or Miss Perfect, finally find the precious person God had for them all along. But it required their laying down of that idol and deciding to embrace the mind of God. If you do that—if you seek the Lord's purpose in your life and open yourself to the prayerful counsel of mature, trusted elders—I assure you that you can find the person God has for you, in His time and of His design.

Guarding My Heart and Mind

> When wisdom enters your heart, and knowledge is pleasant to your soul, discretion will preserve you; understanding will keep you, to deliver you from the way of evil (Prov. 2:10-12).

The most effective route to growth and understanding is to apply the wisdom gleaned from God's Word to our lives. The questions at the end of each chapter will help you examine your own concepts and behavior as well as apply what you have just read to your own situation. To gain the maximum benefit, I recommend that you write the answer to the questions, perhaps in a journal, after giving each question thoughtful, prayerful and honest consideration.

1. What is my reason for being single?

2. How does not being part of a married couple make me feel about who I am?

3. In what specific ways can I, as a single soul, be an effective, ministering agent of the Kingdom?

Father God, I stand on the grounds of Your Word, which exhorts me to be content in whatever state I am in [Phil. 4:10]. I reject any deceiving spirit that would try to attach to my unmarried state a sense of being less than worthy or whole. I thank You that Your beloved Son, Jesus, has set the example for me of how fulfilled the life of a single soul can be, and I embrace that now in His Name. Amen.

CHAPTER 3

Saving Yourself for the One You Love

The Value of Virginity

A once common expression, rarely heard today, contains one of the most considerate declarations of commitment possible: I'm saving myself for the one I love. Those words bring to mind my conversation with NBA basketball great A. C. Green, who stunned the stud- and jock-minded world of sports when, without pretense or self-righteousness, he made known his commitment to abstinence from premarital sex.

A. C., a highly committed disciple of Jesus Christ, was anticipating marriage. Though he was the holder of an NBA championship ring, his will to compete against the spirit of the world made him an even greater winner—even in the eyes of many sports commentators.

We might be hard-pressed in today's culture of excess, extreme and all other forms of X-rated ideas to find many cases like A. C.'s among celebrities. Yet there are those even amid the sophistry and cynicism of a jaded society who honestly admit that a commitment to remain a virgin until marriage is not a sign of religious prudery, social freakishness or a personality devoid of appeal or desirability.

Genuine virginity shatters the fallacious and deceptive idea conveyed by the media's spin on the words "sexually active" and "sexually inactive." The former suggests a vigorous, vital lifestyle; the latter suggests a boorish, passive one. Nothing could be further from the truth. In fact, the passion that drives the commitment of a sexually abstinent person is more accurately described as "active." In this case, a person's actions are aggressively driven by the excellence of a vision for the future and motivated by a vigorous expectancy—the prospect of giving oneself completely *to one person alone* as a gift of wholehearted love.

In contrast, the casual morality that sacrifices the availability of that total gift on the altar of self-indulgence better deserves the term "inactive." Sexually, that "inactivity" is reflected in a passivity toward the idea that a person to whom you offer a lifetime of love deserves the gift that hasn't been repeatedly presented to others. One is reminded of the pop lyric, "I've never been in love before, so I'm very, very sure, no one else could love you more," essentially saying, "I have *more* to give, because nothing's been given away beforehand." The essence of God's idea, which summons us to remain a virgin until married, is one that calls us to respect God, ourselves and our future mate:

> Genuine virginity shatters the fallacious and deceptive idea conveyed by the media's spin on the words "sexually active" and "sexually inactive."

- To *respect God* we understand that none of His laws are designed to *reduce* life, but rather to *fill it* with meaning and to guarantee our long-term best interests;
- To *respect ourselves*, we recognize the worth of our physical beings as deserving more than being handled like marketed goods displayed with the virtual signs: "For sale— Cheap" or "Free! Seal Broken, Handle at Your Own Risk."
- Third, to *respect our future mate* we keep unopened, and protect like a treasure, the preciousness of our deepest

intimacies and the beauty of the most wonderful physical delights two people can ever exchange.

I want to pursue that kind of "active" sexuality as a subject—to examine the value of virginity in the light of God's Word and in the practicality of His ways. In doing this, I am addressing you as a growing disciple of Jesus and, as such, I think it's appropriate to note one added dimension to define the words "saving yourself for the one you love." That is, Jesus Christ our Lord is in this picture too. To keep trust with Him and His ways for your life is to honor Him who first loved us with complete and loving obedience to His call to holiness in His sight.

Saving yourself for Him as the One you love is a biblical concept—not, of course, in the physical sense of sexual relationship, but in the deep meaning of giving your all to His purpose for your life and not letting that purpose get diluted or tarnished by compromise. Understanding the fullness of His salvation gives Him a literal first claim on our bodies (see Rom. 6:12-20; 1 Cor. 6:12-20). We present Him with the highest and best of our devotion and expend our energies only on those things that He approves. To pursue being actively virgin until marriage is simply another way of indicating that, in your life, Jesus Christ is Lord above all.

ANSWERING THE "BUT WHAT IFS?"

With such strong assertions as I've just made, I can imagine there are those who are saying, "It's too late, Jack; virginity is a lost commodity for me now" or "Pastor Jack, I agree, but we are deeply in love, committed to one another, and it seems more and more difficult for us to restrain ourselves. Besides, our marriage is planned and virtually within reach—it seems reasonable to go ahead since we're committed and moving toward a lifetime together anyway."

Believe me when I say that I'm listening. But I also want to say very pointedly to any nonvirgin: Stay with me as we look into God's Word, because it has amazing news for you about your status *now*, as one of His newborn children. To any who are struggling: I know where you're at—I've been there but still not "done that." There are practical and power-filled principles waiting for you in the pages to follow. Please stay with me.

During the five decades of my pastoral ministry, I've talked to and counseled thousands of people who have followed the culture's pied piper of sexual sin and promiscuity only to be forced to pay the piper eventually. I've had occasion to help many people pick up the broken pieces of their lives; these were people who painfully realized too late that God's outlawing of many sexual expressions and intercourse *outside* of marriage is because it destroys people.

But there is good news! The living God not only forgives and restores, but He also is capable of keeping you from stumbling in the first place. He is "able to keep you from stumbling and to present you faultless before the presence of His glory with exceeding joy, to God our Savior, who alone is wise, be glory and majesty, dominion and power, both now and forever" (Jude 24, 25).

THE BIBLE'S CALL TO VIRGINITY

Twenty centuries after the words of the apostle Paul were spoken to the church at Corinth—to believers coming out of (and yet still living in) the pagan culture of their time—his words are just as relevant to us today. Under the anointing of the Holy Spirit, and out of his passion and love for people, this pastor drew a clear dividing line between the way of the world and those who would choose the way of the Lord:

For I am jealous for you with godly jealousy. For I have betrothed you to one husband, that I may present you as a chaste virgin to Christ. But I fear, lest somehow, as the serpent deceived Eve by his craftiness, so your minds may be corrupted from the simplicity that is in Christ (2 Cor. 11:2-3).

To the body of redeemed souls who had committed their lives to Jesus, having once lived so apart from the kingdom of God and His will, Paul declared his desire to present them to God as "a chaste virgin." We could hardly find a time and a people more like our own than that of Corinth—a time so similarly polluted by deception and seduction, and a body of believers so jealously loved by God, who wills that we commit ourselves solely to Him, the One we love.

Most of us understand the forgiveness that is ours through grace when Jesus becomes the Lord of our life; but to those whose past includes sexual violation or sin, it may seem impossible to be considered "chaste virgins." Yet the power of Jesus Christ to purify us before God is so phenomenal that while physical virginity cannot be restored in one who has lost it, transformation in one's mind and attitudes by the inflow of the Holy Spirit *can* effect restoration so that all things become pure to that person (see Rom. 12:1-2). This restoration of our *spiritual* virginity is the miracle of God whose Word declares, "If anyone is in Christ, he is a new creation" (2 Cor. 5:17).

With regard to sex and the single soul, there is an incalculable value to virginity that ensures our Kingdom inheritance and paves the way for a precious treasure of high sexual fulfillment and ecstasy, which God planned for us to enjoy in marriage. I don't wish to alienate people who have lost their physical virginity, as though there is something you can never realize. Yet neither do I wish to transmit the message to a generation of young people looking for fulfillment that the forgiveness and grace available through Jesus Christ means it doesn't matter what you do, because God will forgive you anyway. Romans 6:1-2 tells us otherwise: "Shall we continue in sin that grace may abound? Certainly not!"

The Word of God tells us that our obedience is better than sacrifice (see 1 Sam. 15:22). Jesus' ultimate sacrifice to redeem our lives and restore us as chaste virgins should never be used as an excuse for disobedience to God's directive to value virginity.

THE VALUE OF VIRGINITY

A clear definition of virginity will help us to understand its value. The dictionary defines "virgin" as "a person who has not had sexual intercourse."[1] Virginity is the state or fact of being a virgin, of being sexually pure and inviolate. The word "virgin" is also used to describe territory or land that is unmarred by the hand of man—the magnificence and beauty of unspoiled, unpolluted physical creation around us.

In Scripture there is also a broader sense of the word; it applies to the spirit or soul of a person. In a very real sense, there is a kind of "virginal" purity that is maintained in a relationship between husband and wife, notwithstanding their sexual experience together, because their relationship is unmarred and untainted by that which is outside of God's order. That is what the apostle Paul is referring to when he declares to those believers who have come out of every kind of corrupt and perverted lifestyle that he desires to present them as chaste virgins to Christ.

I believe that when we understand what the Bible says about virginity, our hearts will rise within us with a desire to live that way. Therefore, please look with me at the following 10 statements concerning the value of virginity:

1. Virginity Honors the Wisdom of the Creator's Design and Order

> So God created man in His own image; in the image of
> God He created him; male and female He created them
> (Gen. 1:27).

God has designed men and women with very distinct indicators when it comes to our virginity. In the body of nearly every female there is a small mucous membrane called the hymen that covers the opening part of the vagina and is broken when sexual intercourse first takes place. In most instances, the breaking is accompanied by a small amount of pain and bleeding. According to God's design, a young woman's hymen is a clear physical sign—kind of a "Do not open until Christmas" seal—on her virginity.

The sign that our Creator has designed for a young man is different—it is his inner sense of conscience and awareness. That internal witness is also prompted when solo sex is indulged. It is a law written on the human heart. When sexual sin is first entered into—before one has become calloused by repeated violation—something registers in one's soul. All people—at their first exposure—*do* know when a violation has taken place; it is the subsequent repetition of that violation that numbs their internal witness and eventually begins to justify itself as acceptable.

Virginity is part of God's design and order. Our Creator's signals to honor virginity have been implanted in men and women like warning lights that flash in front of railroad tracks when a speeding train is about to cross its path. God's order is established in His Word—our owner's manual for this body we live in—to preserve and protect us for the true fulfillment He has planned.

2. Virginity Is the Symbol of an Exclusive Allegiance to Jesus Christ

> These are the ones who were not defiled with women, for they are virgins. These are the ones who follow the Lamb wherever He goes (Rev. 14:4).

The book of Revelation gives us a mighty symbolic message that those who keep allegiance with Jesus do not defile themselves with the world's system. In Revelation 14:1-4, we read about a group of people symbolically spoken of as "the one hundred and forty-four thousand." There are two different interpretations of who these people are, and while it doesn't make any difference which interpretation you hold, I believe that it is a symbolic representation of the whole Church, throughout the entire Church Age—people who confront evil in their time, living for God, following Jesus and presenting His life wherever they go. This is a way of thought, a mode of life for people who are serving God in their generation, in their time in history.

In Revelation 14:4, these were not "defiled with women." And then in Revelation 17:15 a "woman" is described—she is the Babylon harlot, and she represents the world-spirit with whom "the kings of the earth have committed fornication" (Rev. 18:3). This doesn't have anything to do with gender; it has to do with the *spirit* people chose to submit to and the way they lived their lives.

The characteristics of the people described in this passage of Scripture are that they "follow the Lamb wherever He goes." In other words, there is an exclusive and total allegiance to Jesus Christ, to do whatever He says. With regard to their allegiance to Him, they are called "virgins." I believe this is a message to those of us who follow Jesus that He's called us to live virginally.

3. Virginity Prizes Purity as a Precious Treasure to Be Preserved and Protected

> For I have betrothed you to one husband, that I may present you as a chaste virgin to Christ. But I fear, lest somehow, as the serpent deceived Eve by his craftiness, so your minds may be corrupted from the simplicity that is in Christ (2 Cor. 11:2-3).

We have already looked at these words from the apostle Paul to the Corinthians regarding his desire to present them as virgins, in purity, before God, and of his concern that they not be deceived or corrupted from the "simplicity that is in Christ." In the original language, the word "simplicity" is more accurately translated as the word "purity." Paul is talking about the simplicity that is unmarred, the purity that is unscathed—that which is not polluted or mixed with other things. In other words, that which is virginal.

Paul was confronting those in the Corinthian church who were tolerating fornication and other sinful behaviors. His powerful words were saying to these believers, in effect, *You can't live that way anymore!* Yet there is a beautiful balance in the way he confronts them without condemning them—as Jesus would, in both absolute authority and unconditional love.

This is the magnificent thing about our Savior. As uncompromising and willing as Jesus is to confront those who have fallen into sin of any kind, our Lord is never condemning. As He was with the woman of Samaria who had been sexually involved with several men she wasn't married to (see John 4:16-18), and the woman caught in the act of adultery (see John 8:11), Jesus' way of confronting is both releasing and delivering to people, while still so clearly persistent to the principles of God's Word.

Sexual purity is a precious treasure to be preserved and pro-
tected. Believers are called to be vessels for honor, "sanctified
and useful for the Master, prepared for every good work" (2 Tim.
2:21). The Bible tells us that the means for achieving that is to
"flee also youthful lusts" (v. 22).

4. Virginity Rejects the Mockery that Treats Innocence as Though It Were Ignorance

> Fools mock at sin, but among the upright there is favor
> (Prov. 14:9).

Our society mocks virginity, flaunting carnal knowledge and sex
by experimentation as the sophisticated and intelligent means
of getting to know one another. Men and women are urged by
today's cultural pundits to find out whether or not they are sexually compatible before committing themselves in marriage.
Sexual self-discipline is often ridiculed as passé and stupid. Yet
how much more stupid is it to engage in premarital sex, risking
the possibility of emotional devastation, pregnancy or even a
deadly disease?

The fact is, engaging in sexual intercourse isn't the only way
you learn about sex! There is much that can be learned before you
ever celebrate your wedding night with the person the Lord gives
you for a lifetime. I can't think of a healthy couple who really love
each other who aren't going to anticipate with high delight their
first night together, though it will only be the beginning of their
sexual relationship, just as growth will need to take place in other
aspects of their married life. Men and women do not need to
enter marriage with a backlog of information; in fact, in many
cases, premarital sex, even between those who later wed, brings an
element of pollution and dysfunction into a marriage, because it
is disobedient to God's Word.

The seduction of singles into having premarital sex is as much a deception as the serpent's tricking of Eve. Mocked for her obedience to respect God's prohibition, she was tricked into believing that God was holding out on something desirable that she and Adam ought to have access to. The fallout was monumental. And the fallout continues to this day.

When it comes to our sexuality, the same satanic spirit of mockery as that which seduced Eve attempts to demoralize and deceive men and women by mocking their innocence as if it were ignorance.

5. Virginity Retains for a Single Beloved One What Is Appropriately Theirs

And he shall take a wife in her virginity (Lev. 21:13).

Consistent from its earliest presentations, virginity is the foundation of all the approaches to marriage spoken about in the Bible. Beginning with Leviticus 21:1-15, it talks about the priesthood getting married, and in Deuteronomy 22:13-30, it talks about the people of Israel getting married. Virginity was so significant to a marriage that its proof was required. In ancient times, the sexual consummation of a marriage took place in a private chamber of the home of the bride's parents. A cloth was provided for the explicit purpose of showing evidence of the bride's virginity by the small amount of bleeding that took place when the hymen was broken. Thus, a legal case could not be brought that would justify the loss of the financial exchange that took place as a result of the wedding. (In other words, they wouldn't have to return the gifts.) If it were found that the bride was not a virgin, all gifts would have to be returned—those were the biblical grounds of approach.

The value of virginity was established in God's order, among God's people, and as a part of their legal system from the very beginning. The Lord puts a high value on virginity; thus, as His people, we are to retain for a single beloved one what is appropriately theirs.

Anna and I have been married for more than 50 years. We married as virgins and have only belonged sexually to one another. We were not without the same temptations that all couples face for the nearly two years we dated before we married. Yet I can attest today that we have found that the preciousness of our life together increases with the passing of every year because of our faithfulness to one another and to the Word of God. Somehow, that accumulates incredible interest, strengthening bonds of stability, confidence and trust, not only in one another but with regard to trust in general in life.

This is why the Lord calls us to virginity: because it retains the possibility for a relationship to be built without any of the pollution or brokenness that corresponds to violation.

6. Virginity Refuses the Notion That Love and Relationship Require Sexual Expression for Fulfillment

Whoever keeps His word, truly the love of God is perfected in him (1 John 2:5).

I want to make clear that the Lord intended for us to have sexual expression and fulfillment in our marriages. But the value of virginity is that it refuses the notion that it is *only* through sex that love and relationship can be expressed. That lie is the fundamental grounds of the appeal, "If you *really* love me, you'll have sex with me." Sex is not intended to be the dominant expression of love in our lives. That doesn't mean that, within the sexual relationship of a married couple, love and affection aren't expressed; but rather it renounces the proposition that it's impossible to express love without sex.

There was no more loving individual in all of history than Jesus, our sinless Savior, who lived His entire life as a virgin. The world's repeated attempt to reduce Jesus to a mere fallible mortal by suggesting that He had a romantic relationship with Mary Magdalene is indicative of its inability to comprehend an expression of love that does not include sex. (Worse, it is a monumental deception perpetrated by the Adversary to defer people from recognizing Jesus as the Savior.) To close the door on this falsehood, we need only state the fact that if Jesus had been sexually involved with anyone, He would have been a sinner, not the Savior. Such an idea reduces the entire message of the gospel to only a legend, leaving us without a Savior and forever lost in our sins.

The Bible says that it was because God so loved the world that He gave His Son Jesus to redeem it (see John 3:16). Our Lord is the most perfect example of the truth that maintaining virginity does not limit one's ability to express profound love in relationship.

7. Virginity Gains Dominion Over Sensuality, Thus Open-ing the Possibility of Highest Sensual Fulfillment

> No good thing will He withhold from those who walk uprightly (Ps. 84:11).

You may need to stop for a minute and think about this statement. How can gaining dominion over something open up the possibility for its fulfillment?

It's the same thing as saying that when we become so desperate for food we will scramble for whatever we can get but never truly experience the pleasure of eating. When desire kicks in, and people seek satisfaction on their own terms rather than on God's, discernment to choose what has been intended by our Creator for our greatest fulfillment is lost. Obedience and discipline make way for investing oneself by *choice*, not out of a response to being stampeded by passion.

Within God's laws and regulations, the Lord wants us to enjoy the complete sensual fulfillment inherent in sex—*in His time* and *on His terms*. Remember, sex is God's invention—including its ecstasies. And the beauty awaiting those who learn the value of virginity is that they will receive every possibility that sexuality affords within God's pure and perfect plan.

Any who submit to being driven by their senses will, in time, find themselves at a profound loss. A case in point is Esau, who, the Bible says, "for one morsel of food sold his birthright. For you know that afterward, when he wanted to inherit the blessing, he was rejected, for he found no place for repentance, though he sought it diligently with tears" (Heb. 12:16-17).

Esau traded the tremendous promise of his inheritance for a dish of stew in the passion of only a single day's hunger. There was never any way of regaining back what was lost to the seduction of a moment's blind desire.

Precious people lose a measure of their inheritance of Christ's authority, dominion and blessing when they surrender to the plea of passion instead of submitting to the perfection of the Lord's will. Jesus calls us to "by . . . patience possess your souls" (Luke 21:19). We have a higher destiny (with promised greater fulfillment) than that which presents itself so desperately in the immediate moment.

8. Virginity Repels the Attempted Invasion of the Soul That Lost Purity Allows

Each one is tempted when he is drawn away by his own desires and enticed. Then, when desire has conceived, it gives birth to sin; and sin, when it is full-grown, brings forth death (Jas. 1:14-15).

The loss of one's virginity by engaging in premarital sex gives place to an invasion of the soul—the mind and emotions—that can lead to bondage. Believers who live in discipleship and obedience to Jesus can still face enormous struggles from past excursions into the unworthy. Let me illustrate.

Some years ago, one of the finest, strongest brothers in our church related to me that he was having horribly impure thoughts and did not know why.

"Jack," he said, "I'm not involved in pornography or infatuation. I'm not doing anything wrong that I know of, yet still I am wrestling with these thoughts."

As we talked, the Lord showed me a picture of him, like an X-ray. In his chest area there were six images that looked like bullets. Attached to each of those were tiny wires. I knew that he had walked in moral purity from the time he was married, and it was after marriage that he had come to Christ. So his sexual disobedience had been outside the Lord.

"This may sound like a strange question," I said, "but before you were married, were there instances of sexual involvement and moral failure?" He answered that there had been. "How many people were you involved with?" I asked.

He thought about it. "Six," he said.

I shared with him what I had seen. Though he was disciplined in his walk with Jesus and would not be dragged by those wires into sin, points of control had been registered in his soul and the Adversary was able to pull his mind there just to assert his evil presence. And to what did those wires attach? Not so much to the six women, but to the spirit that had dominated the moment in which those sinful exercises had taken place.

In another case, a married couple came to our church for

water baptism, and the Holy Spirit revealed to me that they were having serious trouble in their sex life. I pulled them over to the side where nobody else could hear me and said, "I don't want to embarrass you, but I've got to tell you what the Lord just said to me." Upon hearing it, they looked at one another and tears began to fall. They had been married for six months; but for one year preceding their marriage, they had had an ongoing sexual relationship. They had violated the law of God in premarital sex, not knowing that it brings just as deep a bondage as if it had been in promiscuity with others. God's divine program had been inverted, and that cannot be done with impunity.

God's established order is like the law of gravity. If a plane is not following the laws of aerodynamics, then the law of gravity takes over and the plane crashes. Laws of sexual relationship work the same way; they are built into God's creative order. God can't suspend them for us just because we feel we're being so sincere that it ought to be okay. Let me add that in both these cases, confession, repentance and renunciation brought about a restoration of wholeness (see appendix 3).

The enemy of our souls will not cease his attempt to crowd out the possibilities of fulfillment in our lives (see Rev. 12:12). Virginity is a like a shield that repels that invasion because it establishes such an important standard for everything else we allow.

9. Virginity Walks a Pathway That Avoids Contracting Other Polluting Traits of a Decaying World

> But fornication and all uncleanness or covetousness, let it not even be named among you, as is fitting for saints; neither filthiness, nor foolish talking, nor coarse jesting, which are not fitting, but rather giving of thanks. For

this you know, that no fornicator, unclean person, nor covetous man, who is an idolater, has any inheritance in the kingdom of Christ and God. Let no one deceive you with empty words, for because of these things the wrath of God comes upon the sons of disobedience. Therefore do not be partakers with them (Eph. 5:3-7).

There is an enormous value in pursuing the pathway of virginity that extends itself in the lives of believers beyond the preservation of their sexual purity: They are far less likely to become polluted with the other toxic traits of a decaying world.

Here is a passage of Scripture from the eternal Word of God that issues a stern warning: "Let no one deceive you with *empty words*" (Eph. 5:6, emphasis added). The things that "empty words" seduce people into include sexual disobedience as well as "foolish talking and coarse jesting"—the platform of so much of what is presented as entertainment in our society. The Bible says that when these corrupting influences are indulged in by believers "the wrath of God comes upon the sons of disobedience." We are admonished *not* to partake of them.

How many times a day does seduction attempt to deceive us with empty words? No one is going to stop you from going to questionable R-rated movies, or from laughing at the blue humor of a late-night comic. But people who get their minds filled with these kinds of things eventually wonder why they're going sour on Jesus.

What kind of television access do you have in your home? What kinds of magazines do you read? How do you spend your leisure time? Those who value their Kingdom inheritance don't squander it on the unworthy in *any* part of their lives. That which is genuinely fulfilling—as opposed to that which is deceptive, transient and ultimately never satisfying—is found within the order, design and ways of God, our Creator. The pathway of virginity not only preserves a believer, it protects them from contracting other polluting traits of a decaying world.

10. Virginity Exercises a Self-Control that Sustains a Fuller Sense of Self-Worth

> But, beloved, remember ye the words which were spoken before of the apostles of our Lord Jesus Christ; how that they told you there should be mockers in the last time, who should walk after their own ungodly lusts. These be they who separate themselves, sensual, having not the Spirit. But ye, beloved, building up yourselves on your most holy faith, praying in the Holy Ghost (Jude 17-20, *KJV*).

There's nothing like the feeling that you've obeyed the Lord and that His kingdom is dominating your life. With that comes a tremendous sense of wholeness, worth and completeness. It isn't arrogant, vain or proud; it's a very humbling sense of deep-seated authority.

In Jude 18 we read that those who walk in disobedience "separate themselves." It means that as they sin, they literally divide themselves, and pieces of their personality are being sacrificed. Our society speaks more wisdom than it knows when it calls the gaining of a sexual conquest "getting a piece," because that's exactly what happens to the human personality that violates the way of God. The personality winds up in pieces, thereby diminishing a human being's dynamic and worth, and turning them into little more than loose change. Only an inflow of the holiness of God can restore the wholeness needed to put a person back together.

When the apostle Paul wrote to the church at Corinth, he confronted a catalog of gross sinning—specifically listing fornicators, idolaters, adulterers, homosexuals, sodomites, thieves, covetous, drunkards, revilers and extortioners. Having been so categorically specific, almost brutally enumerating the failures—most of them sexual in their violation—he then sweeps in with a marvelous wave of God's grace, adding, "and such were some of you. But you were washed, but you were sanctified, but you were justified in the name of the Lord Jesus and by the Spirit of our God" (1 Cor. 6:9-11). It shouts for all of our attention.

Every stained soul, *listen up!!* That group was the same group of people to whom the apostle later declared his intent to now "present you as a chaste virgin to Jesus Christ" (2 Cor. 11:2). Hear me, please. He would not have said that if he weren't talking about a *real possibility*. In short, the New Testament declares the ability of Jesus to take people who have been sliced up in pieces by inappropriate sexual practices and completely restore them to such wholeness that each single soul can stand before God as a chaste virgin! Of course this doesn't alter the *physical* impact that past sexual practice has had. (In other words, physical virginity isn't the point being made.) What is being affirmed, however, is not only God's love to see us as perfectly pure again in His sight but also God's *power*, which is able to recalibrate our minds, our hearts, our self-respect and our perspective on our sexuality—to *restore a virgin-like mind-set and virginal quality of wholeness to our personalities.*

If there has come bondage through past disobedience, in Christ there is freedom. That freedom comes when we say, "Lord, I renounce all the memories that plague me, all the indulgences I've entertained and all the corruption I've allowed, not only through my body but also in my mind." (A more detailed prayer for renouncing sin can be found in appendix 3.)

Calling our bodies "the temple of the Holy Spirit" (1 Cor. 6:19), the Bible tells us that our lives have been bought at a price—the blood of our Savior, Jesus Christ, who is liberating and transforming us by the power of His Spirit and the truth of His Word:

> Now the Lord is the Spirit; and where the Spirit of the Lord is, there is liberty. But we all, with unveiled face, beholding as in a mirror the glory of the Lord, are being transformed into the same image from glory to glory, just as by the Spirit of the Lord (2 Cor. 3:17-18).

Whether still physical virgins or those who have been spiritually restored by new life in Jesus Christ, God's desire is that every single soul would, from this time forward, preserve themselves for the One they love. Indeed, when it comes to sex and the single soul, the foundational issue of our quest is that of *love* (or our perceived lack thereof). On that topic, the Bible is crystal clear. Love—the deepest, truest and most joyous and fulfilling kind—is inexorably linked to our abiding in God's commandments, as our Lord Jesus tells us in His own words:

> As the Father loved Me, I also have loved you; abide in My love. If you keep My commandments, you will abide in My love, just as I have kept My Father's commandments and abide in His love. These things I have spoken to you, that My joy may remain in you, and that your joy may be full (John 15:9-11).

May you, dear souls, abide in His love and shine with His light as His beloved, joyous children in whom Father God is well pleased.

Guarding My Heart and Mind

1. How has God restored my life to being that of a "chaste virgin"?

2. What do each of the 10 statements concerning the value of virginity mean to me?

3. As a single soul, how can I apply the wisdom of God's Word to the pressures I sometimes feel to surrender to seduction?

Dear Lord Jesus, thank You for the sacrifice You made
in order that my life might be restored to purity before God.
I renounce anything that would corrupt or pollute this
"chaste virgin" and commit my way unto You, for You
have assured me the fulfillment I so long for. I pray
this now in Your heavenly Name. Amen.

Note

1. *Nelson's New Illustrated Bible Dictionary,* Ronald F. Youngblood, General Editor (Nashville, TN: Thomas Nelson Publishers, 1995, 1996), s.v. "virgin."

CHAPTER 4

Discerning the "Rome" in Romance

or What Happens in Vegas Never Stays in Vegas

Sex sells. The inappropriate juxtaposition of humankind's most intimate encounter (sex) with its least personal of transactions (sales) has fueled our culture and marketplace for decades. In turn, it has created false suppositions and confusion about the expectations men and women have about themselves and about each other. No longer highly cherished is the quality of one's character or the depth of his or her commitment to a relationship; rather it is how virile or alluring a "hot" body can be. People are reduced to body parts, and those parts are exploited for the sake of turning a profit. The idolization of sexual magnetism and prowess throttles nearly all of today's media and marketing.

We face a plethora of inappropriate, sexually provocative images throughout our day-to-day world—a reality precisely the same as when New Testament believers first answered their own call to Christ, when Rome's rule and increasing depravity shaped the early definition of "romantic." Perhaps as reflective of the same decaying force in twenty-first-century life is the impact of a greatly productive advancement—the Internet—that also carries such destructive potential. This technology serves us so well in so many ways, but it also seduces multitudes into webs of pornography, corruption and deceit. Good sense, maturity and spiritual discernment are so needed when making choices about our use of the Internet, because when we don't employ these boundaries, then bondage and disaster can ensue at lightning speed.

I have been asked to counsel even accomplished spiritual leaders who have wept before me as they confessed their shame over having become involved in online seduction and invited my help as they sought deliverance. I usually urge them to seek the resource of Christian agencies equipped to lead people through a biblically disciplined pathway to break the addictions that can snare any of us by means of deception. (See appendix 5.)

If any one place encapsulates the relationship between the world's mind-set and seductive temptation, it is Las Vegas—a venue so infamous for the enthronement of avarice and sexual immorality that its nickname is Sin City. But unlike the supposed urbane discretion in the city's recent marketing slogan, *What happens in Vegas stays in Vegas,* the impact of sin upon believers in Jesus Christ registers far beyond one's private world. It ruins families, churches and communities, as character is compromised and the flow of God's kingdom purpose and fulfillment for individual lives is squandered. (You might want to consider the insight and warnings on this subject about which I've written more extensively in my book *Fatal Attractions.*) There is no private world that provides a space in time where sin may be indulged with impunity. Sin will leave its mark or residue upon every relationship we have, "for none of us lives to himself, and no one dies to himself" (Rom. 14:7).

Yet there is hope. Positive trends are emerging among today's Christian youth. Abstinence covenants foster healthy convictions and commitments that help many teens and young adults withstand the onslaught of pressure to engage in premarital sex. As a pastor many years ago exhorted his flock not to be deceived by the world's immoral mind-set and spirit, so it is also my desire to strengthen the hearts and minds of believers who need undergirding in this highly vulnerable area of their lives.

To that end, let us look frankly at a fundamental question I've answered for the full spectrum of age groups—from teens and collegians, to forty- or fifty-something widows, widowers or divorcées who are serious about a relationship that has begun moving toward physical expressions of affection—not to mention some who have already crossed the line of God's wisdom.

HOW FAR IS OKAY?

How far can a couple go to express affection before marriage? What does the Bible say?

Well, the truth isn't hard to find, but the trouble is that the truth so deeply conflicts with the attitudes that surround us in a world living apart from God. I constantly engage in conversation with couples who still struggle with God's counsel—virtually arguing with Him—as I simply seek to offer His protective, instructive, benevolent Word on so tender yet demanding a subject. Let's start with this counsel:

> Beloved, I beg you as sojourners and pilgrims, abstain from fleshly lusts which war against the soul (1 Pet. 2:11).

One of the questions I am most often asked is, What is an appropriate expression of affection during courtship? Any believer who is sincerely concerned about the answer usually concedes the obvious: God absolutely prohibits sexual intercourse before marriage (see Gal. 5:18; Eph. 5:5; Col. 3:5; and Heb. 13:4). The atmosphere of this prohibition is not anti-sex, but *anti-ruin*. Our loving God, creator of marriage's highest physical fulfillment, is only interested in preserving that fulfillment at its *best*. True freedom in pursuing obedience in this regard begins when you and I genuinely believe that.

It is also important to gain a perspective that separates sex from courtship and to keep the focus of a courtship on the building of *relationship* between two people. Inscribe these words on your mind: *Mutual understanding of each other, communication and a relationship built on valuing a person* is what provides the foundational "stuff" for fulfillment (including sexual fulfillment) in marriage. So, then, what can we cite as proper boundaries for expression of affection for an unmarried couple who is serious about one another?

> Mutual understanding, communication and a relationship built on valuing a person is what provides the foundational "stuff" for fulfillment (including sexual fulfillment) in marriage.

WHY SHOULD IT BE LAUGHABLE?

Let's start with the most innocent expression: *holding hands*. No one is going to challenge the holding of hands; in fact, I can imagine that even the mention of so simple an expression can bring a sneering laughter to some who would consider this expression as sexually insignificant. But it's no positive commentary on a society's advancement that the tenderness of touch—of holding hands—could be deemed as meaningless.

There are many societies, even today, in which the touch or holding of a hand is acknowledged as a clear signal of loving intention. It's a sad commentary on our own society that the media has stripped away every expression short of flat-on-your-back-and-naked as being less than love. It would be wise to let that diluted definition speak to us, because when sexual intercourse becomes the definition of love (rather than its most privileged physical expression, reserved for marriage) then we have come to the edge of meaninglessness. Then love, the highest expression of all, has been reduced from meaning *commitment, sacrifice* and *giving* to meaning *transient relationship, self-centeredness* and *taking*.

Please hear me, dear friend. If this strikes you as naive or passé, I'm sorry. My intention is not to say that holding hands is a point of high fulfillment, but rather that it still holds as much potential for meaning for you today as I once experienced it years ago. I'm not a doddering old man; my wife and I have known decades of life's richest fulfillment—including fulfillment in our sexual relationship. But it all began with holding hands—with a dimension of meaning that still brought joy to my heart when I wrote a love poem to her in our forty-second year of marriage titled "Thankful for Your Touch." The following is an excerpt:

> . . . For all my life I'll not forget
>   that day, soon after we had met,
> The first time that you touched my hand,
>   (the "thrill" I felt, you understand!)
> For looking back it's something we
>   now know was something meant to be.
> Remember with me how "one touch"
>   turned out to mean so very much.
>
> Who would have guessed that autumn night,
>   what one brief moment would ignite?
> Collegians walking to their dorms,
>   a dozen of us—true to form,
> All joking, laughing—all in pairs
>   (though boy-girl plans weren't serious cares).
> The "moment" happened as we walked
>   back from the malt shop—as we talked.
>
> Our hands bumped first, and then I dared
>   to take yours in mine. And we've shared

A hundred times since then, the fact
    that somehow in that simple act
Our hearts began to intertwine,
    just as your fingers laced with mine.
(We still hold hands that same way now—
    and still your touch thrills me somehow.)
From that touch, who could know the sum
    of all I'd gain in years to come?
As you've continued at my side,
    supporting me—we've laughed, we've cried.
While times and tides all change and turn,
    along the way one thing I've learned:
You're always "there" to touch my hand,
    to always say, "I understand". . .

                      J.W.H.

Of course, those sentiments—and the balance of those in the rest of the poem not included here—were born at a time when our passions were running at their peak, just like any other young couple. What began for us with holding hands later ran the same risk others face—that of going too far. But confrontation with our own convictions, and a will to invite the Holy Spirit's power to help us preserve ourselves for a marriage not violated in advance, even by us, all resulted in that victory being realized. And in the meantime, holding hands gained a depth of meaning, with a fullness of its own kind of joy, that we would never have discovered apart from the path we chose.

WE MUST REMEMBER THIS: IT *ISN'T* "JUST A KISS"

Some time ago, speaking to a large group of singles, I put a list on the overhead screen that posed "The Evolution of Sensuality Between Persons." I posted it as a part of my presentation and introduced it with this request: "Everybody, I want you to turn to someone next to you and say, 'Look out, the pastor's about to shock us with an outline of his corrupt past!'" Everybody did this, and all were laughing when I then said, "I want to note those things that might mark the pathway from the most innocent to the most consummate of physical *sensual* expressions between people who feel affection for one another." The list read:

- Holding hands, hug and brief goodnight kiss
- Occasions of lengthier embraces and kisses
- Fondling of body parts, extended "wet" kissing
- Actual handling, massaging of genitals
- Virtual or actual sexual intercourse

Many in the room were surprised to hear a pastor be so direct, but there was nothing of silliness among them—there was absolute sobriety and silence, waiting to discover where I was going with this.

My target then was the same as it is here—to answer the question, How far should unmarried couples go—that is, in the light of the Word of God? I didn't take a long amount of time to get there, but began by noting two things: (1) how ridiculous any "progression" appears in a culture where we're so used to seeing TV or film scenarios where everything starts with the last thing on the list; (2) the fact that today the second and third expressions on the list are more commonly one and the same. That's when I ran the risk of sounding like a ridiculous old man— throwing down a challenge for disciples of Jesus Christ who really want to remain virgins until marriage.

In talking with hosts of couples about this, I've found that they say the turning point—where passions overflow most explosively— is at the point of the "wet," "French," or open-mouthed kiss.

As a joyously married man, and as a pastor committed to teach the Word of God and its celebration of celebrative, ecstatic sexual interaction in its biblical context (marriage), I asked the group to open their Bibles with me. As I have so many times, the group was surprised to discover references to open-mouthed kissing in the Scriptures—in the erotic passages of the Song of Solomon (see 1:13-16; 4:1-11; 7:1-10)— a book that is a celebration of two lovers who are overwhelmingly passionate and completely enjoying one another in the physical union of their married love. The book makes two direct references to what is popularly called a French kiss: "Honey and milk are under your tongue" (4:11); and "the roof of your mouth [is] like the best wine" (7:9).

The purpose of noting this is for more than curiosity or amusement; it is to underline—strongly—that the couple in the Bible sharing this joy are married! (See 4:8-12; 5:1.) And on that authority, my firm counsel to all the young people whom I influence and who will listen to me is, "If you refuse to indulge in French kissing until you are married, I guarantee that you'll have an infinitely easier time controlling your passions and maintaining an abstinent stance until your wedding night."

I've never had anyone who respects God's Word mock this counsel, and I've had hundreds upon hundreds of young couples confirm its practicality and apply its wisdom.

Of course, this is "nonsense" to a worldling, and only something I would say to groups or couples who, like you and other readers, I believe will even bother with this book—people who want to be purposeful, power-filled, pure vessels who bear the testimony of Christ as committed disciples of His.

Frankly, Anna and I learned this during the 20 months of our courtship. Early on in our dating as college students who were very much in love with one another and also focused on answering our individual calls to train to pursue church leadership ministry, we struggled with temptation. But when we made a mutual covenant to heed the Word's wisdom in regard to wet kissing, we overcame a hurdle that greatly simplified accepting such disciplines as, for example, refusing to do anything other than embrace and kiss—and to limit the time we allowed ourselves for either. (In this context, "embrace" does not include any handling of breasts, buttocks or genitals.)

The Bible's sole mention of this kind of kissing is, I believe, best understood when we honestly acknowledge the reason why it is mentioned and in what context. Wet kissing involves an actual physical penetration of another person's body—becoming an oral expression of intercourse and a very powerful preparation for that intimacy. There is no way to honestly deny it: This is marriage territory. It is also very unsurprising that such liberty is not only a commonality in today's culture, but it is also aggressively modeled as normal behavior by media. But enough said: I've answered the questions How far is okay? and Where do we draw the line? I leave it with you, hoping that you might be helped by this counsel, just as innumerable couples have told me they were.

Incidentally, with gratitude to God, with humility and with thanks for a girlfriend (later my fiancée) who shared not only my passion but also my greater desire to please God, Anna and I came to our wedding night as virgins. And after five decades together, the joys of marriage and all of its delights continue to this day. We don't believe we missed a thing by waiting.

A PAIR OF DELICATE SUBJECTS

It has been my experience that sincere believers are looking for truth far more often than they are looking for excuses to continue sinning. So as we move farther toward our objective of *sustaining life's purpose through maintaining life's purity,* I want to move into a realm of confrontation that exposes both of us: me to real misunderstanding, and you to the temptation to trivialize the significance of several of today's most commonly excused sexual indulgences—sometimes argued as acceptable for single Christians because they do not involve direct sexual intercourse.

Please keep your focus on my disposition—always non-accusing, patient and understanding. I am neither a legalistic bigot nor a religious prude—I think I've made that clear. But I have presumed what is doubtless true: You are reading this book because you want to know God's Word and liberating truth about how a single soul can find a purpose-filled, fruitful life and not be deterred by the many means with which sexual entrapment ensnares so many.

There are two matters I've learned that both singles and marrieds openly ask, once they discover that I, as a pastor, am not afraid to frankly and openly discuss sexual matters. Among those questions most frequently asked is, What does the Bible say about masturbation?

Honesty with the Scripture requires admitting that masturbation is not directly mentioned in the Bible; but an equally honest understanding of the Greek words employed in the Word, as well as other very clear counsel of exacting calls to disciples, though general in their wording, is instructive. That's what prompted my message, "Solo Sex: Release or Rejection," a CD that has had wide distribution and elicited constant favorable response (see Appendix 5). I have elaborated much of this message in my book *The Anatomy of Seduction* and consequently feel no need to repeat the same here. But let me make brief mention as follows.

First, I grieve that a few Christian authors propose that masturbation is nothing more than a necessary biological release. While this is true of wet dreams, self-stimulated ejaculation is another thing. I withstand the idea that the fact that a believer is a biological being should ever be posed against the fact we are foremost a spiritual being. This isn't an argument for mysticism or suggesting that we're supposed to be, or act, less than human. But it does remind me that to live and walk in the fullness of God's Spirit who dwells in my physical temple is to answer my call to progressively grow away from the carnal-mindedness and habits of a world mind that provoke or philosophize the indulgence of my flesh.

I have not suggested that masturbation is a satanically inspired activity and certainly deny that it will in itself damn a soul or separate a believer from God's love. But it is a matter of yielding to the flesh and confronts thoughtful disciples with three facts.

1. *It is a surrender to sensuality*—submitting to the flesh, to one's body's desires, in the face of God's call to deny ourselves and take up the Cross and follow Jesus.
2. *It is a surrender to fantasy*—submitting to lewd imaginations and adulterous thoughts: it never takes place in a mental vacuum.
3. *It is a surrender to deception*—pretending that none of these things makes any difference, when Jesus says they do (see Matt. 5:28).

To conclude with this oft-inquired matter, let me summarize:

• While this practice neither separates a believer from Christ nor conclusively denies his or her *intent* to grow as a disciple (even to overcoming such a habit), it is nonetheless a proven opponent of our spiritual, emotional and mental maturity.

- What is legally tolerable for a believer and what is prag-
matically and spiritually advantageous are two different things: "All things are lawful for me, but not all
things are helpful; all things are lawful for me, but not
all things edify" (1 Cor. 10:23). Serious discipleship has
to answer the question, Is this something I can imagine
Jesus seeing as edifying?

The candor needed to strongly urge anyone confused on
such a topic runs to the edge of awkwardness. I am not anxious
nor find it particularly desirable to explore such a theme, but it
becomes essential, seeing that so much confusion is rampant.
My feeling of awkwardness is not because I doubt the truth of
my counsel, which is rooted in God's Word, but because I want
to help you toward *growth*.

"IT'S NOT *REALLY* SEX . . . "

The second "delicate subject" I've referenced above concerns a
matter not publicly discussed until the past decade. Today our
culture has virtually equated sexual gratification with mental
health, treating abstinence and self-discipline as peculiarities
rather than normal and desirable. It is in this environment that
questions (usually written confidentially) are regularly asked of
me concerning oral and anal sex.

The impact of the press coverage of a former United States
president's dalliances not only seemed to normalize oral sex, but
for hundreds of thousands of children who would not even have
encountered the thought of it until they were older, it has
birthed problems of perversion, brokenness and even disease
that rock sectors of our society at this very moment.

Years ago, I prepared a brief statement on this subject to
answer the question that many *marrieds* posed to me in times

of counsel (see appendix 4). I leave it to you to weigh this as an expression within the bonds of marital union, but I want to make this much clear right here: *This expression is out of bounds for singles*—at least on God's terms. Like mutual masturbation, the idea that anything short of a full and actual consummation of sexual intercourse is "not really sex" is a delusion born of a culture gone wild—a culture with a badly damaged moral compass.

ARE THESE INDULGENCES FORGIVABLE?

The answer is "Yes—of course they are!" And with that, let me emphasize that *nothing* in these pages is intended to breed condemnation, but rather to call believing singles to a life consumed with God's purpose for them rather than a culture's permissiveness.

In answering questions biblically, I still refuse to set myself up as a self-righteous critic or to resource anyone who might attempt to take my words and use them as a whip—legalistically damning or attacking people for their sexual failure.

Jesus hasn't changed: He came into the world, *not* to condemn the world, but that the world through Him might be saved, forgiven and delivered (see John 3:17). *All* sexual sins are forgivable, but let me encourage you that we should always think humbly, as recipients of God's grace: Just because your or my sin may be readily forgiven should never make it a matter of casual concern to us.

Wherever and whenever a seeking heart wants to become an understanding one, I believe that we, as believers in Jesus, are always obligated to reveal the loving heart of God to that person, irrespective of how broken, confused, tormented or weak he or she may be. Jesus says, "All that the Father gives me will come to Me, and the one who comes to Me I will by no means cast out" (John 6:37). We are all sinners in need of the Savior, and our acceptance of each other should be based on those terms.

However, *acceptance* of a person should not be equated with *approval* of sin or a supposition that sin doesn't make any difference. This distinction—between acceptance and approval—has become blurred of late, both in our culture and in the Church. Let's grow forward—as disciples who choose to "lay aside every weight, and the sin which so easily ensnares us" (Heb. 12:1), refusing to be chained by any fleshly indulgence, however approved it may be by the world-spirit dominating our culture.

Guarding My Heart and Mind

1. What is the reason behind Father God's commandments with regard to our morality?

2. Knowing that our culture glamorizes sin, what influences or behavior have I habitually given place to or justified in my life?

3. What effect does sexual indulgence, either solo or between singles, have upon a future relationship?

Father God, thank You for the clarity in Your Word with which You have established the boundaries of Your protection, as well as the blessings of Your promise, over my life.
I surrender my heart to You this day, and I reject the seducing, deceiving spirits of this world that would reduce all that You made me to be to nothing more than body parts.
I stand firm in the liberty with which Christ has made me free, praying in Your Son, Jesus', matchless Name. Amen.

CHAPTER 5

How to Live and Love in a Perverted World

Understanding God's Heart and Discerning His Word

We've navigated some of the greatest challenges to a *purely powerful, purposeful life as a disciple*. Now let's turn a corner and discuss applying that power as a servant and witness for Jesus in our broken world. This is the objective of holy living—why we have been begotten to newness of life. You and I have been saved to be shaped as agents of Christ's kingdom—to shine His life, love and light into a darkened culture blinded by sin and doomed to death.

To become a loving, life-giving representative of the Savior in a morally confused and oft-perverted world requires growing in the truth and spirit of Christ. It calls us to a balance gained by an internal moral stability. It also calls us to a compassionate availability that will enable a genuine, discerning capacity to love and accept sinners, while refusing to accept anything of the ruinous ways, standards or behavior of a sin-blinded world. It means being stretched past bigotry and prejudice and becoming able to graciously relate to people who are living in moral darkness in the same way we would gently relate to a blind person who is lacking physical eyesight. To illustrate this balance, let me tell you about Richard.

Richard's Story

It had been nearly two years since Richard had come to Christ. His transformation by the power of the gospel and his rediscovery of the Creator's true design for him as a person—as a man—had produced a true disciple of Jesus. The pathway out of his former lifestyle of living in the West Hollywood community with his male lover had been more than an experimental excursion. As a professional in the medical community, he was respected for his skills. As a member of the homosexual community, he was accepted by a broad circle of like-minded friends. He was the consummate example of all that any community would want to designate as a case study for its effectiveness. In essence: He's a success, and he's one of us!

The situation changed rapidly, almost viciously, when Richard received Jesus as his Savior. The rejection he experienced had nothing to do with reasons a critic might presume. He became neither a self-righteous judge of his friends nor a preachy saint. But he explained himself to his lover and made every effort to assuage wounded emotions when he announced that he would be discontinuing their relationship. "I care about you, Charles," he said. "But honesty with the truth, and faithfulness to the love of God for both of us will not allow me to live as I have anymore. I don't want you to feel I hate you or think you are an unworthy person. I simply know God has a better way for both of us."

The reaction was explosive.

Charles was furious and immediately spread the word that Richard had more than simply "done him bad," he had become one of "them." In the view of hosts of gays, "them" represents those in the Christian community who appear to devalue the humanity of anyone embracing homosexuality. Many do not resent Christians' faith as much as they resent what they regard in many Christians as a loathing, demeaning judgment of them as people. They perceive the epithet "abomination" as a hate-filled, condescending announcement laced with a social intolerance of individual human rights and motivated by a quest for political control that would exterminate them if Christians ever gained governing power.

Now Richard had become one of "them."

Richard's regret was not rooted in the speed with which his many friends turned their backs on him or in the bitterness that virtually spit at his new life of commitment to Christ. Rather he was brokenhearted over the twisted perception of his former friends in knowing what Jesus is really about, and he was equally regretful for the few cases of supposed "Christian" activity that justified the caricature drawn of "them." That is what had brought about our meeting in my office.

Richard had written me a letter of warm encouragement. He described his having found our church after his conversion to the Savior, and he expressed his deep gratitude for the atmosphere as a haven of hope. He wrote,

> Pastor Jack, it hasn't been easy to find a fellowship that offers both grace and truth. I wanted to say how thankful I am for a congregation that is constant in both: (1) a commitment to God's Word and its requirements for living in God's will (including the call away from sexual disobedience) and (2) a commitment to God's love and its requirements for showing God's grace to the lost (including a generosity of spirit to all who live in a blindness to their sin—seeking to "love them to life" rather than viewing them with condescension).

I was more heart-warmed by his discerning, solidly discipled understanding than I was by his nice remarks about our church.

He was a marvelous case of the way that Jesus saves. Those two words that summarize the gospel—"Jesus saves"—were in full evidence in this man who had been completely transformed, resurrected from a deadly environment and who now walked steadfastly in the light of God's Word—a man who was compassionately concerned about those he might reach for Christ, especially those in the grip of his former confusion. Those reasons were heartwarming enough, but I was about to discover something even more profoundly heart stirring.

Our conversation was concluding when Richard made a request. "Before I go, Pastor Jack, would you mind praying with me about something that's happening right now?" I nodded my head, inviting him to go on. "I want to ask your prayer support for the next few days. Let me explain."

He outlined briefly how, only a few weeks before, he had received word that his former lover was dying—now under the siege of a virulent assault of AIDS. Hearing that Charles had virtually disappeared, Richard went to the apartment they had formerly occupied together and found him there. "I knocked on the door, not only wondering if he was there at all, but also feeling very uncertain of what kind of reception I would find if he was.

"When the door cracked open, I was stunned. His faced was shriveled: He had open sores, and he looked like walking death. As he peered at me through squinting eyes, his expression turned to a scowl. He seemed uncertain about opening the door and weakly said, 'Oh, it's you.'"

Richard explained how Charles had then turned away from the door, leaving it open behind him. "If I hadn't had the medical training I do, it would have been dangerous to go in, but I followed him."

The apartment was in disarray and the stuffiness of the room unpleasant with the smell of death encroaching upon a human body. Richard said nothing but went about cleaning the place as Charles returned to his bed. With the caution and skill of a professional, Richard proceeded to attend to Charles's needs—helping bathe, cleansing the sores, remaking his bed, and then preparing a meal for him.

"There were few words exchanged," Richard said. "He was so desperately in need, he could hardly protest the help I was offering. And when I finished washing the dishes, I told him I would be back the next day. Pastor Jack, that was nearly four weeks ago, but my request for prayer is because of what happened this week."

I was already near tears as I listened. The manifest purity of Richard's motives, the gracious compassion in his actions, the clear-eyed concern in his words to me—all were the essence of a Christ-like forgiving nature. Here he was, reaching where he had been rejected, loving in the most practical of terms and with the purest of objectives.

"In all these weeks of ministering help to Charles, Pastor, I intentionally did not mention Jesus even once—not because I am ashamed of Him, but because I knew it wouldn't be received. And then, just three days ago, as I was helping Charles back to bed after changing the sheets, he said, almost with pitiful resignation, 'Okay, Richard. Tell me about Jesus.'"

Both Richard's and my eyes were misted as he described how Charles opened his heart to the Savior. And I was overcome with this evidence of the power of forgiveness when it is shown toward the very person who has rejected you.

The request was direct: that we pray for Charles's last days on Earth. Neither Richard nor I were devoid of the belief that Christ can heal, at times even in the most extreme circumstances. And neither of us doubted the possibility of willingness within the mercy of God for one whose condition was the result of a clear violation of His benevolent intent for mankind. But there was a sense of closure—one that Charles had expressed, and one to which Richard bore witness—that the physically tormented body about to be left behind was no longer the definition of Charles's future. He had received the Savior. He was ready to go. So, we prayed. Two weeks later, another redeemed soul entered eternal glory, and Richard phoned me to report Charles's homegoing.

CALLED TO BALANCE RIGHTEOUSNESS WITH LOVE

Richard's story models a balance greatly needed in today's Church. He faced the brokenness produced by the world's hollow notions that God's order may be disregarded with impunity. Sin's destructiveness is not a direct judgment from the Almighty but an invited self-destruction given place to through disregard of the warnings God's love gives us against those things that destroy.

I believe we're looking at a call to the Church today that requires us to learn how to live and love in an increasingly perverted world. The term "pervert" is sometimes invoked in a sneering manner, but what I have to say is completely the opposite of that. "Perversion," of course, is a biblical term, and it refers to anything that is adverse to the created order. Perverted things are those that have become the *reverse* of what God would have. In arguing for the *reverse*, a prevailing attitude becomes *per*verse. It is manifest in any way in which any practice or lifestyle proven to break hearts and ruin bodies is not only philosophized as worthy but is also self- or socially legitimized, seducing or recruiting others to those ways.

Among so many moral exclamation marks punctuating our world, arguing against values that followers of Jesus hold dear, some of the most difficult questions disciples face today are, How should I relate to homosexuality? to same-sex marriages? to pro-abortion interest groups? to any group or citizen who is radically different from me or radically belligerent against my values?

As inconsistent as these practices may be with God's laws, they do not license my becoming hateful in the name of righteousness. And as disappointed or vexed as I may be when any of these practices become accepted (and possibly legalized) in my community, I am all the more called to learn how to reach without anger and to love without self-righteousness. At the same time, I am charged by God's Word to retain and live in line with His Word and His righteous ways.

The problem is, we cannot impose our ways or will on a blinded world. Our call is to learn to "become blameless and harmless, children of God without fault in the midst of a crooked and perverse generation, among whom you shine as lights in the world" (Phil. 2:15).

How can we live and love in an increasingly decaying world? I believe there are keys to help us open the doorway to reaching and rescuing people, rather than shaming or slapping them with words or attitudes that may reflect righteous convictions but fail to reveal righteous love.

> Among so many moral exclamation marks punctuating our world, some of the most difficult questions today are, How should I relate to homosexuality? To same-sex marriages? To pro-abortion interest groups? To any group or citizen who is radically different from me or radically belligerent against my values?

THE KEY TO UNDERSTANDING GOD'S HEART

With reference to contemporary morality, probably no text is more quoted than the first chapter of Romans. It tells us about the massive dimensions of God's love when received as revealed, and it warns us of the frightening price of rejecting that love. A catalog of deeds is listed, noting the deepening corrosiveness they beget when persistently pursued as:

- A *conscious choice* to reject or suppress truth (see vv. 18-20)
- A *refusing choice* to neither worship nor thank God (see vv. 22-23)
- An *arrogant choice* to exalt one's own wisdom and to deify nature (creation) rather than Creator (see v. 25)

Verse 16 to the end of the chapter is the frequently quoted passage of Scripture that describes the increase of decay that takes place in an individual and in a society when the revelation of God is renounced. We live in such a society today—one that, by reason of its pluralization, is experiencing paganization. More and more we are living in a Godless culture that is considerably distant from the God-fearing culture of only a half century ago in which there was an esteem and regard for biblical, moral values.

Today we deal in a society that knows little or nothing of those values, and the only thing that will speak to it is the evidence that our lifestyle and love afford—revealing a worth that people value more than anything else. It is not the value of our truth (however valid), but the value of our love. Where people see love being lived out, in time, many will inquire into the truth that produces that kind of life.

WE ARE AGENTS OF GOD'S LOVE, NOT HIS WRATH

It is an illusion to suppose that we win the world by *information*. Rather, we are sent into the world to win it by *incarnation*—by the beauty, power and grace of Jesus, the Savior who was condemned by the religious people of His day for eating with publicans and sinners.

It's possible that there are readers of this book who have had some relationship to the homosexual lifestyle, even perhaps who are participating in it. In indicating the grace that I believe a disciple of Jesus is to show toward a worldling, it is important that I not mislead you. If you are involved in homosexuality (or any other form of sexual expression outside the boundaries of God's Word, as we have already discussed), you may wonder how God feels about you. I will tell you how He feels: *He is furious* (see Rom. 1:18-32). But please understand this: God's anger is not so much a fury born out of His being *offended* as it is born of a passion that violently hates anything that would deceive you out of what He *intended* for your life. God's *whole Word* is before you with a *wholeness of life* that will heal and deliver as greatly as it will forgive and save you from any self-destructive counterfeit that has been presented and sold to you.

And to each companion disciple of Jesus who, along with me, lives in a wholehearted quest to do His will in all things, we are wise to learn of that quality of love that so passionately honors God. While I oppose that which destroys, my passion toward humanity must reveal that dimension of His love the worldling can comprehend. It is imperative to recognize that we have been made ministers of God's love to the world, not agents of His wrath. It is His role to exercise judgment—your and my role is only to live with discernment.

THE KEY TO DISCERNING GOD'S WORD

After Romans 1, Leviticus 18 is frequently quoted in reference to those perversities often argued as legitimate in our world today. One word most noted is "abomination."

The term itself contains such thunder that the case seems closed at once; but without contesting the truth that abomination (detestable) is exactly what God means here, it is—as always—pivotally important to hear God's heart and to see precisely where His Word was being addressed in this text.

In the first five verses of Leviticus 18, the Lord is essentially saying that He has brought them out of Egypt and is bringing them into Canaan. Freely paraphrased, God says to His own people, Israel,

> I brought you out of a lifestyle where everything in the world had the touch and taint of the idolatrous and self-indulgent. Now I'm bringing you into an environment where the residue of these people is polluted with the satanic, the evil, the most distorted and the wicked. While you are My people, and I've delivered you out of the bondage of Egypt, I'm not bringing you into a pure, wholesome environment; I'm bringing you into a place where *what you are in My Name* will make the difference.

Hear the heart of God in this passage of Scripture—He isn't speaking to a pagan culture but to His own people under His covenant, saying, *I am insisting that you live a life that works, not participate in the hateful death-syndrome of a dying culture!*

Yes, God's Word does declare a host of perverse behavioral and sexual practices of mankind as being morally abhorrent, and my part is to teach that He has said it. But it isn't my assignment to pass judgment on those outside God's covenant—it's my mission to tell them of the redemptive possibilities of His saving grace.

They'll hear me best when I reveal His love and reach to them with His works!

GOD LOVED US WHILE WE WERE YET SINNERS

The call of the Scriptures always is redemptive and preserving in its focus. It is not about our saying to the world, *You keep these rules and God will love you.* To the contrary, the Bible says that "God demonstrates His own love toward us, in that while we were still sinners, Christ died for us" (Rom. 5:8). And in John 3:16, "God so loved the world"—unconditionally, unqualifiedly—"that He gave His only begotten Son." No regulations imposed upon the world. Jesus said in John 8:15, "I judge no one."

Jesus came executing no judgment, but reached in love. That doesn't mean He had no discernment or that He was indiscriminate or promiscuous in the conduct of His own life. It means that He was not here to raise up a standard for people to rise to, but to reach with the long arms of God to draw people in; and that in those people who came to Him, something of the recovery of what God had in mind as a standard for humanity might be manifest so that others would desire it. Not that they would take the searchlight of their newfound righteousness and shine it in the eyes of the unregenerate, saying, *See how corrupt you are? When you get over the glare, maybe we'll help you out of the dark.* Rather, that light was to examine their own lives and to so warm the presence of love in their own midst that it would attract other people out of the darkness.

This is the key to understanding not only the heart of God, but also the Word of God. And when we understand and grasp that key, holding it well in hand, then something of His enormous power, grace and transformation will take place—and our agent-role as ministers of His life, light and power will find effective entry.

Guarding My Heart and Mind

1. What do I honestly think my response would be if a gay or lesbian couple visited my church and sat down next to me?

2. What in my own life has become or has ever been compromised in any way, opposing God's order? How
   might remembering that keep me equipped with
   humility to minister in wisdom and grace?

3. In what ways can I shine the loving light of Christ in
   the darkened areas of my community among my
   friends and acquaintances and even within my family?

*Dear Lord, forgive me for where I've fallen short in
extending Your love toward others. Show me how to see the
world through Your eyes, to love the world with Your heart, and
to shine the light of Your life, drawing people out of the darkness
and into Your glory. In Jesus' Name, I pray. Amen.*

CHAPTER 6

The Purposeful, Spirit-filled Single

Living with God's Heart—Holding
Fast to God's Word

In the light of God's Word, and with the love of God's heart, we (that's every single soul) who desire to live a purposeful, Spirit-filled life need to *review* our concepts and *renew* our compassion. That means that your and my concepts need to frame a behavior based on His Word, and our compassion needs to be fired with a frustration with ourselves, rather than a frustration with the worldling for not being what he or she ought to be. The key to our living with God's heart—to pump His flow of grace, love and compassion into a broken, wounded (and sometimes hostile) world—is squarely centered on the practice of reviewing our attitudes.

ASSESSING OUR ATTITUDES

Believers in Jesus Christ cannot expect a society set against the Creator to understand our insistence that it acknowledge His will for human behavior. Too many sincere Christians, especially in North America, suppose that today's playing field is on the same level as that of the pre-1960s, when the historic traditions undergirding our nation's values system more readily acknowledged a basis in God's Word. Not only is the percentage of Bible-believers lower today, but people also face a basic disposition to challenge anything simply because it's in the Bible. State and federal court cases challenge historic traditions (including but not limited to public prayer and display of Scripture), yet many Christians who are understandably disappointed, if not frustrated, by this, suppose we still have the same grounds of appeal as in the past.

In confronting these mistaken "grounds" for our objections, I am not yielding to the intrusion of corrosive values or the anti-religion advances in our world. I'm simply saying that unless we posture a more realistic way of relating to our culture as it is now, rather than as we wish it would be, we neutralize our own capacity to effectively communicate with people whom we would hope to win to Christ.

> The only power that will penetrate the culture as a whole is the dynamic of Spirit-filled intercessory prayer as you and I target issues before the face of God rather than in the face of a blinded world.

Contrary to the thought of some, I don't see our foremost assignment from Christ as trying to change a culture, but rather as seeking to reach individuals with the life and love of Jesus. That is not to negate our privileged role as citizens to speak into our society, nor to suggest that we be politically passive. Rather, it's to keep our priorities straight at a time when "right wing" seems to be the definition of "righteous," instead of being "right on" in our mission to evangelize.

So make no mistake: I'm not shouldering an agenda that supports or is casual about those who oppose historic tradition and biblical values; I am just saying that we need to get real regarding our call as believers in a perverse world.

WE ARE NOT CALLED TO MEASURE THE WORLD BUT OURSELVES

It is easy to be misunderstood as indifferent about the moral drift in our society in saying this, but please understand: God has not assigned the Church a mission to call the world to meet a moral standard. He has called the Church to live a moral standard!

Yes! Every human soul will have to answer to God regarding their moral behavior. Yes! Leaders in government will be held accountable by the Almighty for how they led or failed to lead righteously. But asking a world that is dead in sin and blinded to God's Word and values to act as though it were alive and possessed with a clear view of God's ways is like beating a dead horse—to rant at its lifeless carcass, give it the whip and hope it will win the Kentucky Derby. In short, we can't measure the world or expect it to toe the mark and measure of God's Word when we ourselves—who are alive in Christ—can only hope to do so by the grace and power that we've received through new birth. A dead world can't answer a call to live without being brought, one by one, to Him who is the Resurrection and the Life.

So our primary resources for changing our world are the following: (1) being filled with the Holy Spirit, so the love of God overflows our lives in all contact, communication and relationships (see Rom. 5:5); and (2) recognizing that the only power that will penetrate the culture as a whole is the dynamic of Spirit-filled intercessory prayer made effective as you and I target issues before the face of God, rather than in the face of a blinded world.

THE WARFARE THAT CAN WIN

I do believe that we are engaged in warfare for a culture—for our society and the millions in it! But where and with whom we battle is my point of concern, and my plea is for a contingent of single believers who will engage that war with understanding.

Ephesians 6:10-12 is perfectly explicit in drawing the line between a culturally concerned Christian who makes people and politicians their adversary, and those who recognize the manipulative conspiracies of the power of darkness. Principalities and powers and the cohorts of hell listed in that text are not only real, but they are also dynamically and deceptively powerful. However, interceding believers, empowered by Holy Spirit-filled and assisted prayer, can break the dominion of the Adversary's dynamism and neutralize His success at deceiving those who are lost, blinded and dead. I want to enlist a battalion of spiritually active singles, discipled with the Word's wisdom and anointed with the Spirit's power, to form prayer teams and groups that live in and love our perverted world with the one form of activism that can change it.

> Therefore, I exhort first of all that supplications, prayers, intercessions, and giving of thanks be made for all men, for kings and all who are in authority, that we may lead a quiet and peaceable life in all godliness and reverence (1 Tim. 2:1-2).

In 1 Timothy 2, the Early Church was called to pray for a government that was totally corrupt and for leaders who were known to be homosexuals. Strikingly, the text doesn't leave room for us to choose to pray only for those of our own political affiliation. Those governmental, judicial or societal leaders who represent us in our respective parts of the nation may have radical, if not corrupt, differences of opinion from us. And while I may exercise my privilege to vote against them, and use my voice in a free society to express my feelings with sensitivity with regard to what I have said above, I am still mandated by God to pray for them. Hear me: You cannot effectively pray for anyone you hate, and you can't speak to God for their transformation while at the same time you speak unkindly about them to people around you.

The summons to be the people of God calls all of us, then, to assess our attitudes. I need to learn how to be a good neighbor as well as a good citizen. And above all, I need to live out God's love with a graciousness of attitude, even to people who are the antithesis of every value I hold. I also need to learn how to be a faithful intercessor, committed to fight where the victory can be won—not against flesh and blood, but against the demonic spirits whose grip can be broken where effective prayer warfare is waged by the living Church.

HOLDING FAST TO THE WORD OF GOD

As we draw to a conclusion, let me emphasize that you and I must keep our heads and hearts centered on a lifestyle rooted in the Word of God. Let me highlight two final points of focus—points to underline in His Word, our mind-set and our lives.

1. Commit to Living and Loving Within Your Family (see 1 John 2)
Within our families, we need to help our loved ones understand how to think clearly on moral subjects without cultivating the attitude that homosexuals are damned. It's not a matter of validating the homosexual agenda but of helping family members sort out the truth in their minds. This can be done by responding to those points of biblical understanding that I have laid out in this book and by growing in the discerning life, thought and love that understanding will engender. Cultivate within your family a climate rich in the resources of spiritual discernment and loving discipline, and teach morality on the basis of its promise and hope, not as a system of fear and taboos.

2. Shine as Lights in a Crooked and Perverse World (see Phil. 2)
In speaking to the people of Philippi in ancient Greece, an area known not only for its tolerance but also for its advocacy of an amoral lifestyle, the apostle Paul wrote the words we examined earlier (see Phil. 2:14-15). These words call us to a spiritually proactive posture rather than an attitudinally reactive one. Reexamine his counsel that is put in such a magnificently beautiful way, calling believers to "shine as lights"—that is to let the glory of God that shone in the face of Jesus Christ shine in you. Dear one, let's go for it! Let's shine His light into our workplaces, communicate it to our neighbors, reach with it to unsaved relatives—all with a sensitivity that refuses to condemn and that commits to live the light in a way that warms and wins!

As we do, let's watch for people who manifest a hunger for spiritual reality. The Holy Spirit knows who they are and He'll cause you to cross paths with them. I predict, possibly to your amazement, that you may find that some of those people will be ones you have heretofore seen as ardent advocates of everything that is disapproved or distasteful by the standards of God's laws. Still, our tactics are those He has commanded: Go and proclaim the good news! And the fact is, the Good News isn't a set of legal requirements issued from heaven, but the graciousness and love of the living God who sent His Son from there—who sent Him to us, and who now sends us to others.

It is my prayer that the sweep of the Holy Spirit would settle on the heart of every single soul reading this book, softening and preparing it for the Lord's harvest in our world. Stand firm on the Word of God! But also make your stand as one whose heart has been warmed by God's love and whose attitude has been tempered by remembering that it was grace, not law, that brought us to our blessed Savior.

Go forward in that grace!

Holy Spirit, I invite You to remove any hardness from my heart or perverted notions that I have held about what God's Word says. Thank You for Your forgiving grace through Jesus Christ and for the true identity and destiny You've ordered for my life. Make me an instrument of Your radiance—a beacon of light that will warm and draw multitudes. I pray this now in the name of Jesus, my Lord and Savior. Amen.

A Prayer for Receiving Christ as Lord and Savior

It seems possible that some earnest inquirer may have read this book and somehow still never have received Jesus Christ as personal Savior. If that's true of you—that you have never personally welcomed the Lord Jesus into your heart to be your Savior and to lead you in the matters of your life—I would like to encourage you and help you to do that.

There is no need to delay, for an honest heart can approach the loving Father God at any time. So I'd like to invite you to come with me, and let's pray to Him right now.

If it's possible there where you are, bow your head, or even kneel if you can. In either case, let me pray a simple prayer first and then I've added words for you to pray yourself.

MY PRAYER

Father God, I have the privilege of joining with this child of Yours who is reading this book right now. I want to thank You for the openness of heart being shown toward You and I want to praise You for Your promise, that when we call to You, You will answer.

I know that genuine sincerity is present in this heart, which is ready to speak this prayer, and so we come to You in the name and through the Cross of Your Son, the Lord Jesus. Thank you for hearing.[1]

And now, speak your prayer.

YOUR PRAYER

Dear God, I am doing this because I believe in Your love for me, and I want to ask You to come to me as I come to You. Please help me now.

First, I thank You for sending Your Son, Jesus, to Earth to live and to die for me on the cross. I thank You for the gift of forgiveness of sin that You offer me now, and I pray for that forgiveness.

Forgive me and cleanse my life in Your sight, through the Blood of Jesus Christ. I am sorry for anything and everything I have ever done that is unworthy in Your sight. Please take away all guilt and shame, as I accept the fact that Jesus died to pay for all my sins and that through Him, I am now given forgiveness on this earth and eternal life in heaven.

I ask You, Lord Jesus, please come into my life now. Because You rose from the dead, I know You're alive and I want You to live with me—now and forever.

I am turning my life over to You and from my way to Yours. I invite Your Holy Spirit to fill me and lead me forward in a life that will please the heavenly Father.

Thank You for hearing me. From this day forward, I commit myself to Jesus Christ, the Son of God. In His name, amen.[2]

Notes

1. Jack Hayford, *I'll Hold You in Heaven* (Ventura, CA: Regal Books, 2003), pp. 38-39. Used by permission.

2. Ibid., pp. 39-40.

A Prayer for Inviting the Lord to Fill You with the Holy Spirit

Dear Lord Jesus,

I thank You and praise You for Your great love and faithfulness to me.

My heart is filled with joy whenever I think of the great gift of salvation You have so freely given to me.

And I humbly glorify You, Lord Jesus, for You have forgiven me all my sins and brought me to the Father.

Now I come in obedience to Your call.

I want to receive the fullness of the Holy Spirit.

I do not come because I am worthy myself, but because You have invited me to come.

Because You have washed me from my sins, I thank You that You have made the vessel of my life a worthy one to be filled with the Holy Spirit of God.

I want to be overflowed with Your life, Your love and Your power, Lord Jesus.

I want to show forth Your grace, Your words, Your goodness and Your gifts to everyone I can.

And so with simple, childlike faith, I ask You, Lord, to fill me with the Holy Spirit. I open all of myself to You to receive all of Yourself in me.

I love You, Lord, and I lift my voice in praise to You.
I welcome Your might and Your miracles to be manifested in
me for Your glory and unto Your praise.

I'm not asking you to say "amen" at the end of this prayer, because after inviting Jesus to fill you, it is good to begin to praise Him in faith. Praise and worship Jesus, simply allowing the Holy Spirit to help you do so. He will manifest Himself in a Christ-glorifying way, and you can ask Him to enrich this moment by causing you to know the presence and power of the Lord Jesus. Don't hesitate to expect the same things in your experience as occurred to people in the Bible. The spirit of praise is an appropriate way to express that expectation; and to make Jesus your focus, worship as you praise. Glorify Him and leave the rest to the Holy Spirit.

A Prayer for Renouncing Sex Sin and Inviting Deliverance

PRAYER

Heavenly Father, I come to you in the Name of Jesus. I come with repentance and humility to receive the cleansing I need. I believe the Blood of Jesus cleanses me from all sin. Holy God, I desire cleansing and freedom from all sexual sin and impurity and all unholy soul ties.* I confess and repent of my own sexual sins and of the sexual sins of my former generations.**

I specifically confess as sin and I repent of giving place to sexual lust: lust of the eyes, lust of the flesh, impure thoughts and all sexual fantasies.

I repent for all involvement with any kind of pornography. I specifically repent of the viewing or use of pornographic photos, books or magazines, pornographic movies, computer pornography and Internet chat rooms.

I repent of all involvement in the sins of fornication, adultery, infidelity and prostitution. I repent of all involvement in perverted sex, including homosexuality, sodomy, sadism, orgies, group sex and sexual activity with animals.

Heavenly Father, I specifically repent of all attitudes and all words or actions forcing or requiring my spouse to participate or take part in any sexual acts which to them are degrading and distasteful or that violate their conscience before God.

I repent of sexual self-gratification and self-indulgence, including masturbation, exhibitionism and Internet or telephone sex. I also repent of all attitudes, actions and spirits associated with sexual pride, sexual power, sexual conquest, enticement and seduction.

And now, Father God, I renounce*** all these sexual sins: all sexual immorality, fornication and adultery, lust of the flesh, perversion, pornography, sexual abuse, selfishness and manipulation. I renounce all unclean spirits behind these sins. I renounce all unholy soul ties. I want nothing more to do with them or with any sexual sin, in the Name of Jesus.

In the Name of Jesus, through the power of the Holy Spirit, I break the yoke of bondage from all sexual sins. I choose from this moment on to walk sexually pure before my God.[1]

DEFINITIONS

*Soul Ties

A mental or emotional attachment of the soul to a person or object, involving both the mind and emotions, resulting in the influencing of the choices of our will.

There are *good soul ties* (see Gen. 2:24; 44:30; Deut. 10:20; 1 Sam. 18:1 and 2 Sam. 20:2) and *destructive soul ties* (see Gen. 34:1-3; Num. 25:1-3; Josh. 23:12-13 and 1 Cor. 6:16).

**Generational Ties

> Keeping mercy for thousands, forgiving iniquity and transgression and sin, by no means clearing the guilty, visiting the iniquity of the fathers upon the children and the children's children to the third and the fourth generation (Exod. 34:7).

Although the sins of former generations are not credited to our account, there is still something very destructive that takes place. If the sins of our parents are unrepented of, the spiritual influence behind those sins tends to press in on us in the next generation (i.e., children of abusive parents are more likely to succumb to abusive behavior in their own life).

***Renouncing

> The night is far spent, the day is at hand. Therefore let us cast off the works of darkness, and let us put on the armor of light (Rom. 13:12).

> And have no fellowship with the unfruitful works of darkness, but rather expose them (Eph. 5:11).

An action taken by the believer in Jesus Christ against the forces of darkness that declares all previous association to be cancelled. All words, agreements or actions that opened the door to demonic influence are now broken.

Note
1. With thanks to Pastor Chris Hayward, President, Cleansing Stream Ministries. Used by permission.

Regarding Questions About Oral and Anal Sex

First, let me set the context for even bothering with so delicate a subject as this. And let me emphasize: *This is a book for singles*, not a handbook on the marriage relationship. So why write about such intimacies (or corruptions, depending upon the reader's point of view)?

My only reason for speaking to the matters addressed here is that many singles have been either married or exposed to sexual involvement that has already put this issue on the table of their past. Consequently, within the pursuit of a present or future relationship, it is possible that they may be indulging in these ways, somehow supposing this isn't really sex. The reader will find here the depth of my convictions and explanations; obviously, some may take exception to my views—these opinions are offered because I am asked, not because I open the subject. The following is divided into two sections: (1) our present cultural context, and (2) my pastoral counsel to marrieds on the matter. At the end, I have made clear that my views, while strongly felt, are not arrogantly proposed. I hope this addendum helps those with significant questions on these matters.

OUR PRESENT CULTURAL CONTEXT

Given the preoccupation of today's culture in which sexual gratification has become a substitute goal for true sexual responsibility, integrity and highest marital fulfillment, questions are regularly asked of me concerning oral and anal sex, including questions about the personal or partnering use of devices designed to artificially stimulate or substitute for normal sexual intercourse. Rather than deal with this within the body of this book, I am offering in this appendix the essential counsel I have provided when couples voluntarily inquire of me regarding oral sex. My remarks presume an understanding that practices associated with sexual perversion are not intended for humankind, nor are they biblically supported.

By "oral sex," I refer to the practice of the mouthing of the penis (fellatio) or vagina (cunnilingus). The greatest delusion, exacerbated in its influence by the impact of the widely read affair of a U.S. president in the 1990s, is that oral sex has been suggested by some unmarried believers as a means of preserving chastity. Further, oral sex has come to be broadly regarded within society as not really sex but simply an exercise of personal choice without sexual implications. This is a bizarre interpretation of a very sexual practice, trivialized to the point of ridiculousness.

At least in the U.S., the years since that national humiliation have seen this deception infecting like a virus the mind-set of the culture, not so much because the claim was credible but because our saturation with the subject had the effect of neutralizing any sense of ready willingness to challenge the moral questionability of the practice. Long advanced through pornography, and as a sensual novelty always reaching through human curiosity for exploratory excursions by those whose fancies were snared, oral sex has become virtually normalized as expected practice—not only in marriage but also in general "romantic lovemaking." In the wake of the press coverage of the above mentioned affair, sociologists and educators have reported that an alarming number of middle school- and high school-aged teenagers have begun regular practice of this expression; this has not only advanced the demise of innocence in our culture but also has perpetuated the belief that they were not performing a sexual act. In a nationally televised interview with parents (*The Oprah Winfrey Show*), moms and dads described how their teens define oral sex as simply another way to relate, "like a kiss," that "it's no big deal, because everybody's doing it." The parents went on to explain that this act is sometimes openly performed in view of other kids.[1] The peer pressure to act out in this degrading manner also reveals the disturbingly low self-esteem of so many young girls in today's society.

As a thought-provoking sidebar to the issue of sexuality among teens, a study released in 2003 by the National Campaign to Prevent Teen Pregnancy concluded that adults underestimate their influence on teens and that teenagers want more advice from their parents on sex.[2] But questions about oral sex (and masturbation) are so frequently asked of our church's pastoral staff by both married believers as well as by engaged couples that the readiness of many of today's parents and churches to answer teens' questions seems sadly lacking—both of convictions about and of commitment to teaching people about sexual self-discipline. Private counsel with these individuals and couples too often turns up deep personal problems stemming from these inordinate practices.

PASTORAL COUNSEL OFFERED TO MARRIEDS

Marriage is honorable among all, and the bed undefiled; but fornicators and adulterers God will judge. Let your conduct be without covetousness; be content with such things as you have (Heb. 13:4-5).

The perversion that has overtaken our society with practices and lifestyles akin to homosexual behavior ought to be a concern for believers seeking to pursue a godly relationship within their marriages. Both oral and anal sex are now considered fairly acceptable behaviors within marriage. Yet I have never been in a counseling situation in which I've found that either of these practices contributed to the fulfillment of the marriage. Instead, I have dealt with many, many cases in which they have distracted from the highest satisfaction of the husband and wife's union.

The Bible does not specifically say that oral and anal sex are disallowed in a marriage relationship. But in Hebrews 13:4, it does say that the marriage bed is to be *kept* "undefiled"—a mandate stating that couples must preserve their love life, not only for one another, but also free of the world's corrupting influence. For example, pornographic videos are not to model lovemaking for a believing couple. The world's preoccupation with orgasmic gratification at any cost is opposed to the biblical model of sexual fulfillment begotten in a climate of honor, mutual devotion to one another, loving communication and even fiery passion. The call given to believing couples in Hebrews 13:4 to practice the self-imposed discipline of keeping their marriage lovemaking untainted by the cheap ways of the world is *not* suggesting something less than high desire or a united, joyful spontaneity in a couple's lovemaking. Rather, it is a call—even within the freed and freeing arena of the married sexual relationship—to maintain vigilance against anything that gradually introduces impurity and ultimately reduces vitality. So it is that the New Testament instruction points married disciples to a sensitivity and availability to the Holy Spirit's promptings to *keep their marriage bed (i.e., sexual intimacies) unpolluted*—free of the things that dissipate that pure energy for the preciousness of the face-to-face communication and overwhelming ecstatic and satisfying union our Creator designed this aspect of our humanity to enjoy.[3]

Sexual communication within a marriage is equally as important as verbal communication. Throughout my years of pastoral ministry, I have found that wherever there is a breakdown in communication with a married couple, it virtually always traces back in some way to an absence of a mutually satisfying sexual relationship. The intimacy of a husband and wife's sexual relationship—its act of complete self-disclosure, mutual surrender and unselfish giving—is the heart of the marriage relationship.

In that regard, warm and loving communication is probably best symbolized in the face-to-face union of a couple in the intimacy of intercourse. "Inverted posturing" tends to distract from a depth of communication possible between a married couple in lovemaking. This may be why the majority of times I have dealt with this question (always at the request of couples, not on my initiation) the wife is so often uncomfortable with the practice— often urged by the husband, not against her will but involving more a concession on her part than a preference. This, of course, has not been uniformly the case, but given the greater inclination of women to want "communication" while men too often focus on "stimulation," we are probably at the foundational reason for this difference of feeling about oral sex within marriage.

God made our bodies to relate to one another in sexual union in a way that is distinct from all the rest of creation: We're created to face one another. I don't want to seem tawdry in saying this, but a man has two hands that desire to touch a woman's two breasts. Lovemaking, kissing face-to-face and seeing each other eye-to-eye provide the far deeper possibility of expressing affection to *a person,* making it much more likely that a man and woman will truly be *together as one* than if they resort to the interplay of mouth-to-genitals stimulation. I propose that in the Creator's ingenious gift of our human capacity for sexual fulfillment, the soul-to-soul *visual and speech* capacities that communicate affection, devotion and fidelity are far and away the most profound and fulfilling aspects of sexual union—joined, of course, to the physical interaction of normal intercourse.

I am not espousing a prudish attitude toward lovemaking in marriage; that is, for example, I do not endorse the world's mocking stereotype that says only the "missionary position" is acceptable for Christians. I am, however, suggesting that beyond the evidence of the Scripture's challenge to resist the invasion of the world-spirit into our intimate lives, the dignity of the husband-wife relationship recommends face-to-face enjoyment of each other, as opposed to the ease with which oral sex may play toward investigating anal sex. The latter is an animal position rather than human, and thereby not only dehumanizing to a woman but also painful, bringing the possibility of injury and infection.

These observations are not an attack on a person or persons' faith in Jesus but are intended to *help answer questions when they are asked.* They may, however, result in thoughtfully asking ourselves if there are ultimately issues of personal ethics: Are these practices that strengthen and deepen your marriage relationship or debase and depersonalize it? I am convinced that these matters deserve to be challenged, but not necessarily condemned. The vast majority of the time I have had feedback from inquiring couples regarding these matters, they have been relieved and released: (1) freed from ideas they have found in sex guidebooks suggesting their sexual relationship would be incomplete without this, or (2) helped by discovering that one mate was not really happy with such practices but still conceding for fear of seeming unloving or unresponsive. My inclination has been to believe the prompting of the Holy Spirit to be the source of their inquiry, as He seeks to nurture health, wholeness and fulfillment in every believer—even in a married couple's sexual enjoyment.

Let me conclude with this caveat: The Bible does not speak conclusively on this subject. Neither do I believe that I am the final arbiter of what a loving, married couple may choose for their own marriage love and play. I do not reject someone who disagrees with my particular viewpoint, but I have learned from years of counseling couples that many are puzzled or are in disagreement regarding this. Others have, with the passing of time, discovered that these practices have netted a weakening of their sexual desire for one another because a mate has become preoccupied with "tricks" rather than true intimacies. Thus, I have written this for a couple to discuss together—emphasizing that I never want to appear to preempt something they mutually have found meaningful. By that I mean (1) that they have agreed on this form of lovemaking as an accepted part of their expression to one another, (2) that neither partner makes a demand of his or her partner over the wishes and comfort level of the partner, and (3) that these expressions do not become a substitute for normal sexual expression, though they employ them as a part of their foreplay.

Beyond all, I advocate that the Holy Spirit, not the world-spirit, be given place in our hearts and minds to sustain purity, passion and health in the marriage union as He assists us in sustaining our values and keeping all our practices governed by God's wisdom and graciousness.

Notes

1. "Let's Talk About Sex" from the show "Children Left Home Alone," *The Oprah Winfrey Show,* ABC-TV, January 14, 2004.
2. Kate Zernike, "Teenagers Want More Advice from Parents on Sex, Study Says"; *The New York Times,* Dec. 16, 2003. http://www.teenpregnancy.org /about/announcements/news/pdf/NY%20Times%2012-16-03.pdf (accessed March 30, 2004).
3. "Let your marriage be held in honor in all things, and thus, let your marriage-bed be undefiled." K. S. Wuest, *The New Testament: An Expanded Translation* (Grand Rapids, MI: Eerdmans Publishing Company, 1961), p. 536.

Lenski translates Hebrews 13:4 as "Honorable let marriage be in all respects, and the bed undefiled" and then comments, "The imperative is in place. Marriage is to be kept *HONORABLE*" (emphasis added). R. C. H. Lenski, *The Epistle to the Hebrews* (Minneapolis, MN: Augsburg Publishing House, 1966), p. 471.

Word Biblical Commentary makes this observation: "The literary form [is] . . . set forth as direct imperatives . . . 'it must be respected' [that is, marriage]; 'it must be undefiled' [i.e., the marriage bed]." The grammatical structure is formulated with the force of an imperative. William L. Lane, *Word Biblical Commentary*, vol. 47 (Dallas, TX: Word Books, 1991), n.p.

Suggested Resources

BOOKS BY JACK HAYFORD
RELATED TO THEMES IN THIS BOOK,
AVAILABLE AT WWW.REGALBOOKS.COM

Other volumes in The Sexual Integrity Series

Fatal Attractions: Why Sex Sins Are Worse Than Others

Receive the biblical wisdom and practical application necessary to bring hope, healing and restoration from sexual violation.

The Anatomy of Seduction: Defending Your Heart for God

Protect your spiritual integrity through this biblical guide that provides real-world solutions for avoiding seduction of the mind and body.

Living the Spirit-Formed Life—The Ten Disciplines of Spirit-Filled Living

Believers committed to growth and fruitfulness in Christ will be greatly assisted by this extensive guidebook to discipleship. Discover and advance your life in the power and blessings of those basic disciplines proven to build deep, strong and steadfast spiritual living.

Resources mentioned in this book and suggested to allow further inquiry on demanding themes. Available at www.jack hayford.org or by calling toll-free (800) 776-8180

Solo Sex: Release or Rejection (CD/Audiocassette)

> A message brought to thousands who, knowing the subject of masturbation was to be dealt with candidly and biblically, attended with earnestness, not curiosity, and responded with overwhelming gratitude for the clarity, honesty and biblical soundness it reflected.

Biblical Perspectives on Divorce and Remarriage (CD/Audiocassette Album)

> In ministering for decades to a congregation among whom there are those coming to Christ from a broken marital background, Pastor Hayford and the elders of the church constantly utilize this resource to answer questions and address issues of historic legalism—still providing a strong call to Bible-based recovery and restoration on the terms of New Testament discipleship. Two-message album includes, Can God Put Together What Man Has Split Asunder? and Divorce and the People of God.

Other Resources by Jack Hayford (also available at www.jack hayford.org)

Manifest Presence: Expecting a Visitation of God's Grace Through Worship (book)

> Hayford's most recent book on worship—introduced at the 2005 Hillsong Conference in Australia at which he spoke—leads readers into discerning the difference between personal or corporate worship that enters God's presence and approaches His throne with purpose, as compared with the dangers in misinterpretation of worship's purpose. This book offers points to refine and retain the reader's availability to the present renewal of worship in the Church.

Grounds for Living (book)

> "Perhaps Jack Hayford's most important book" was the assessment made by one of today's most effective leaders and church planters. A practical study that establishes "doctrine as dynamic, not boring or static" this handbook for every Christian unfolds and underscores those foundational truths critical to a steadfast walk with God.

The Beauty of Spiritual Language: Unveiling the Mystery of Speaking in Tongues (book)

> Discover the biblical basis for the place of tongues in a believer's prayer life. Pastor Hayford dismantles the doubts that confuse speaking in tongues as either mere gibberish, superficial

emotionalism or disordered exuberance, and provides exposition of God's Word that gives practical understanding concerning this aspect of intimate encounter with the heart of God in prayer.

Calling Men Out (DVD)

Two extended messages for men: How to Think Straight About Women (in order for a man to think straight about himself); and How to See Straight in the Invisible (in order to function as a man of spiritual discernment and functionality in God's kingdom today).

When Kingdom Rules Don't Count Anymore (DVD)

Emphasizes the biblical priority and accountability of a leader's faithfulness to his or her marriage. Confronting the contemporary slackness toward marital fidelity, this teaching provides a baseline requirement for church leadership and sifts through shallow ideas that refuse the responsibility to restore fallen leaders rather than offer a cheap "forgiveness" that is neither releasing nor truly restoring.

Honest to God (CD/Audiocassette)

A classic on walking in the light as disciples of Jesus who walk in integrity and openness with fellow believers and with God. Contains two messages: Integrity of Heart and Singleness of Eye.

The Finger of God (DVD)

A discussion of and introduction to the nature of spiritual bondage as it invades and dominates sectors of the believer's person, attitudes or thoughts. Notes Jesus' words "If I by the finger of God cast out devils" as characterizing that aspect of His ministry that overthrows bondage imposed by satanic opposition and breaks strongholds where the Adversary has been given a place by human carnality. (Includes 50-page booklet with diagrams as a clarifying aid to studying this theme.)

Internet Resources for Education and Support

Jack Hayford Ministries (www.jackhayford.org)

The King's College and Seminary (www.kings college.edu)

Cleansing Stream Ministries (www.cleansing stream.org)

NARTH (National Association for Research and Therapy of Homosexuality) (www.narth.com)

Focus on the Family (www.family.org)

Also in the Sexual Integrity Series

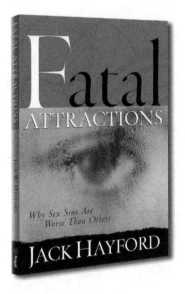

Fatal Attractions
Why Sex Sins Are Worse Than Others
Jack Hayford
ISBN 08307.29682

Real-world tools of biblical wisdom and practical application necessary to bring hope, healing and restoration from sexual violation to any sincere person seeking God's will for his or her life.

The Anatomy of Seduction
Defending Your Heart for God
Jack Hayford
ISBN 08307.29690

Be prepared with real-world solutions when temptation knocks, readied to defend with spiritual integrity, empowered with truth and enabled to keep the focus centered on God.

More from Jack Hayford

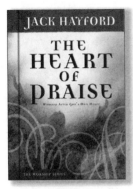

The Heart of Praise
Worship After God's Own Heart
Jack Hayford
ISBN 08307.37855

The Christmas Miracle
Experience the Blessing
Jack Hayford
ISBN 08307.25180

**Living the Spirit-
Formed Life**
Growing in the 10 Principles
of Spirit-Filled Discipleship
Jack Hayford
ISBN 08307.27671

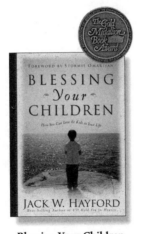

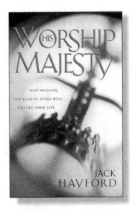

I'll Hold You in Heaven
Hope and Healing for the Parent
Who Has Lost a Child Through
Miscarriage, Stillbirth, Abortion
or Early Infant Death
Jack Hayford
ISBN 08307.32594

Blessing Your Children
How You Can Love the
Kids in Your Life
Jack Hayford
ISBN 08307.30796
VHS • UPC 607135.008422
DVD • UPC 607135.008491

Worship His Majesty
How Praising the King of Kings
Will Change Your Life
Jack Hayford
ISBN 08307.23986